W9-CEI-891

PS
3523
O46
C3837
1994

Tavernier-Courbin,
Jacqueline.

The call of the
wild.

52012

$23.95

DATE		
2 2 MAR 2000		

DISCARDED

CHESAPEAKE COLLEGE
THE LIBRARY
WYE MILLS,
MARYLAND 21679

BAKER & TAYLOR

THE CALL OF THE WILD

A Naturalistic Romance

TWAYNE'S MASTERWORK STUDIES

Robert Lecker, General Editor

THE CALL OF THE WILD

A Naturalistic Romance

Jacqueline Tavernier-Courbin

TWAYNE PUBLISHERS • NEW YORK
Maxwell Macmillan Canada • Toronto
Maxwell Macmillan International • New York Oxford Singapore Sydney

Twayne's Masterwork Series No. 142

The Call of the Wild: A Naturalistic Romance
Jacqueline Tavernier-Courbin

Copyright © 1994 by Twayne Publishers
All rights reserved. No part of this book may be reproduced or transmitted in any form
or by any means, electronic or mechanical, including photocopying, recording, or by
any information storage and retrieval system, without permission in writing from the
Publisher.

Twayne Publishers   Maxwell Macmillan Canada, Inc.
Macmillan Publishing Company   1200 Eglinton Avenue East
866 Third Avenue   Suite 200
New York, New York 10022   Don Mills, Ontario M3C 3N1

Library of Congress Cataloging-in-Publication Data

Tavernier-Courbin, Jacqueline.
    The call of the wild : a naturalistic romance / Jacqueline Tavernier-Courbin.
      p.   cm.—(Twayne's masterwork studies ; no. 142)
    ISBN 0-8057-8081-5—ISBN 0-8057-4458-4 (pbk).
    1. London, Jack, 1876–1916. Call of the wild. 2. Adventure stories, American—
History and criticism. 3. Wolfdogs in literature. 4. Wolves in literature. 5. Dogs in
literature. I. Title. II. Series.
PS3523.046C3837   1994
813'.52—dc20   94-14565
                                                                          CIP

The paper used in this publication meets the minimum requirements of American
National Standard for Information Sciences—Permanence of Paper for Printed Library
Materials. ANSI Z3948–1984. ∞ ™

10 9 8 7 6 5 4 3 2 1 (hc)
10 9 8 7 6 5 4 3 2 1 (pb)

Printed in the United States of America

Contents

053870

Illustrations

Jack London

Reproduced by permission of the Henry E. Huntington Library, San Marino, California

Note on the References and Acknowledgments

I decided to use the Penguin Classics paperback edition of *The Call of the Wild*, which is readily available and affordable (*"The Call of the Wild," "White Fang," and Other Stories* [New York: Penguin Classics, 1987]). This small volume also includes three other stories: *White Fang*, which is generally considered as a companion, if antithetical, story to *The Call of the Wild*; "Bâtard," an outstanding story which might well be described as an anatomy of hatred between man and dog—the very story the violence and cruelty of which London intended to redeem in *The Call of the Wild*; and "Love of Life," another brilliant story which is not particularly related to *The Call of the Wild*, except perhaps in the passionate love of life it dramatizes.

I want to thank the Henry E. Huntington Library, San Marino, California, for granting me permission to reproduce two photographs: one of Jack London taken in 1900 and one of the Bond Dawson cabin, showing, on the left, the dog Jack whose great qualities and personality inspired the character of Buck in *The Call of the Wild*. I also want to thank the Huntington Library for permission to quote from unpublished manuscripts in its collection.

I am grateful to the Social Sciences and Humanities Research Council of Canada for a grant that allowed me to complete the research and the writing of the book.

Chronology: Jack London's Life and Works

1876   Born 12 January, the son of Flora Wellman, who names as his father William Henry Chaney with whom she had lived as common-law wife in 1874–75. On 7 September, Flora marries John London, and the child is renamed John Griffith London.

1878   After Jack and Eliza, his stepsister, suffer nearly fatal attacks of diphtheria, the family moves across San Francisco Bay to Oakland where John London runs a grocery store and sells produce to the local markets.

1881   The family moves to a farm in Alameda.

1882   Jack starts grade school in Alameda.

1886   The family buys a house in Oakland after having lived on two different farms.

1891   Jack graduates from Cole Grammar School (eighth grade) and begins working in a cannery. A few months later he purchases the *Razzle-Dazzle* with money borrowed from his nanny, Virginia Prentiss, and becomes an oyster pirate on San Francisco Bay.

1892   Serves for nearly a year as a deputy patrolman in the Fish Patrol of San Francisco Bay.

1893   Ships as an able-bodied seaman aboard the *Sophia Sutherland* on an eight-month seal-hunting expedition in Hawaii, the Bonin Islands, Japan, and as far north as the coast of Siberia. From this comes his first publication, the prizewinning essay "Typhoon off the Coast of Japan," published in the *San Francisco Morning Call* on 11 November. In late August, he takes a job in a jute mill at 10 cents an hour for 10 hours a day.

1894   Works as a coal heaver in the power plant of Oakland. In April, he joins "Kelly's Army"—a group of unemployed men marching to Washington to protest economic conditions. Leaves Kelly's Army at the end of May and begins tramping on his own. Serves a prison term for vagrancy in Erie County Penitentiary (29 June–29 July). After his release, he tours the East Coast and returns west by coal-car across Canada, earning passage from Vancouver on board the SS *Umatilla* as a coal stoker.

1895   Attends Oakland High School, publishes some short stories and articles in *The High School Aegis*, and falls in love with Mabel Applegarth.

1896   Joins the Socialist Labor Party in April, leaves high school, crams for the entrance examination at the University of California, and attends university for one semester.

1897   Takes a job in the Belmont Academy laundry. On 25 July, sails for Juneau, Alaska, with his brother-in-law, Capt. James H. Shepard, on board the SS *Umatilla* and then on board the *City of Topeka*, and joins the Klondike Gold Rush. Spends the winter on Split-Up Island, eight miles from Dawson City.

1898   Suffering from scurvy, he returns from the Klondike, rafting down the Yukon River from Dawson to the Bering Sea, arriving in Oakland in late July. Begins serious writing.

1899   Devotes all time and energy to writing, publishing 24 items, including stories, essays, poems, and jokes; in particular, "To the Man on Trail," published in the *Overland Monthly* (January 1899), and "An Odyssey of the North," in the *Atlantic Monthly* (January 1900). Meets Anna Strunsky in December.

1900   Feeling the need to settle down and have a family, he marries Bessie Maddern on 7 April. *The Son of the Wolf* is published.

1901   Birth of his first daughter, Joan, on 15 January. Defeated as a candidate for mayor of Oakland. *The God of His Fathers* is published.

1902   Lives in the East End of London, England, during August and September, among slum dwellers, collecting material for *The People of the Abyss*. Travels in Europe for three weeks to recuperate. Birth of his second daughter, Bess, on 20 October. *A Daughter of the Snows*, *Children of the Frost*, and *The Cruise of the Dazzler* are published.

1903   Falls in love with Charmian Kittredge and is separated from Bessie. Purchases a sloop, the *Spray*, to sail on San Francisco Bay. *The Kempton-Wace Letters* (philosophical love letters written in collaboration with Anna Strunsky), *The Call of the Wild*, and *The People of the Abyss* are published.

1904   War correspondent in Korea for the Hearst Syndicate covering the Russo-Japanese War from January to June. Bessie files for divorce on grounds of desertion, naming Anna Strunsky as cause of separation. *The Faith of Men* and *The Sea-Wolf* are published.

1905   Spends the summer at Wake-Robin Lodge in Glen Ellen, Sonoma County. Purchases 129-acre ranch (6 June), the beginning of his Beauty Ranch. In October, he begins a Socialist lecture tour of the East and the Midwest. Marries Charmian on 19 November, the day after his divorce from Bessie is final. Honeymoons in Jamaica and Cuba. *War of the Classes*, *The Game*, and *Tales of the Fish Patrol* are published.

1906   Returns from honeymoon on 11 January and resumes lecture tour on 19 January. Begins building the *Snark*, for his intended seven-year around-the-world cruise. Reports the Great San Francisco Earthquake (18 April) for *Collier's*. *Moonface and Other Stories*, *White Fang*, and *Scorn of Women* are published.

1907   After numerous delays, the *Snark* finally sails for Hawaii on 23 April, arriving a month later. *Snark* drops anchor in Pearl Harbor on 20 May, needing extensive repairs. Jack and Charmian visit the Hawaiian Islands. Sail for the Marquesas Islands on 7 October, and later Tahiti, arriving on 27 December. *Before Adam*, *Love of Life and Other Stories*, and *The Road* are published.

1908   Round trip from Tahiti to Oakland aboard the *Mariposa* to sort out finances (13 January–14 February). Resume *Snark* voyage on 4 April, when they sail for Samoa, then for the Fiji Islands, the New Hebrides, and the Solomon Islands. Leave the Solomons on 4 November for Sydney, Australia, where he is hospitalized for a double fistula operation and also suffering from assorted tropical diseases. (For a long time, the *Snark* has been a hospital boat for all passengers.) *Snark* voyage officially abandoned on 8 December. Purchases La Motte Ranch, adding 110 acres to Beauty Ranch. *The Iron Heel* is published.

1909   Jack and Charmian leave Sydney on 8 April on the English tramp ship *Tymeric*, returning to Oakland via Ecuador, the Panama Canal, New Orleans, and the Grand Canyon, and arriving in Glen Ellen on 24 July. Jack sails the San Joaquin and Sacramento river deltas on board the *Phyllis* (17 October–9 November). *Martin Eden* is published.

1910 Jack begins in earnest the development of Beauty Ranch, purchasing the 700-acre Kohler-Frohling-Tokay Ranch, thereby expanding his ranch to nearly 1,000 acres. Birth and death of his first daughter with Charmian (19–21 June). Purchases the *Roamer* to sail the San Joaquin River delta. *Revolution and Other Essays*, *Burning Daylight*, *Lost Face*, and *Theft: A Play in Four Acts* are published.

1911 Sailing trip aboard the *Roamer* on San Francisco Bay (11 April–3 May). Drives a four-horse wagon with Charmian and Nakata (his servant) through northern California and Oregon, a 1,340-mile return trip (12 June–5 September). Moves from Wake-Robin Lodge to Ranch House on Kohler Ranch. *When God Laughs and Other Stories*, *Adventure*, *The Cruise of the Snark*, and *South Sea Tales* are published.

1912 Signs publishing contract in New York City with the Century Company (30 January) and a five-year contract with *Cosmopolitan* for fiction (5 August). With Charmian, sails from Baltimore on 1 March for a five-month voyage to Seattle around Cape Horn on board the *Dirigo*. Soon after their return to California on 4 August, Charmian miscarries their second child (12 August). Jack buys Freund Ranch, which connects with Kohler Vineyards, increasing Beauty Ranch to approximately 1,400 acres, and begins building Wolf House. *A Son of the Sun*, *The House of Pride and Other Tales*, and *Smoke Bellew* are published.

1913 Discusses a movie contract in Los Angeles with the Balboa Amusement Producing Company (24–30 April), which ends in December by a copyright trial ruling in Jack's favor. Resumes publishing in June with Macmillan, and in July he is operated on for appendicitis. Wolf House burns to the ground on 22 August, a fortnight before completion. Only the mortgage is insured, and Jack is now heavily in debt. (Arson is suspected.) Begins cruising the San Joaquin and Sacramento river deltas (18 October). Meets Ed Morrell (11 December) to hear his prison story—material that will be used in *The Star Rover*. *The Night Born*, *The Abysmal Brute*, *The Valley of the Moon*, and *John Barleycorn* are published.

1914 Continuation of *Roamer* cruise and trip to New York City (January–February). Correspondent for *Collier's* magazine in Mexico (18 April–18 June), covering the American intervention in Vera Cruz. Charmian and Nakata accompany him.

Departs on new *Roamer* cruise on 4 October. *The Strength of the Strong* and *The Mutiny of the Elsinore* are published.

1915   Winter Carnival at Truckee (15–17 January) and return to Glen Ellen (31 January). Jack and Charmian depart on 23 February for a five-month stay in Hawaii on the *SS Matsonia*. Return to Glen Ellen 23 July. Sail again to Hawaii on the *SS Great Northern* on 16 December. *The Scarlet Plague* and *The Star Rover* are published.

1916   Jack and Charmian return from Honolulu on the *SS Matsonia* on 26 July, arriving in Glen Ellen on 3 August. Encounters legal problems over water rights (October–November). Ruling is in his favor. Dies of uremia, complicated by a self-administered dose of morphine to help ease the pain of renal colic, on 22 November. Recent medical evidence suggests a heart attack as the direct cause of death. *The Little Lady of the Big House*, *The Turtles of Tasman*, and *The Acorn Planter: A California Forest Play* are published.

LITERARY AND HISTORICAL CONTEXT

Bond Dawson cabin, 1898. Marshall Bond, dog Jack (the model for Buck), Oliver H. P. LaFarge, Lyman Colt, dog Pat, Stanley Pearce. Above the door the sign reads *Saint Anthony Club*, a club at Yale University to which the Bond Brothers belonged. This photograph is a modern print from the original glass negative, which has disappeared.

Reproduced by permission of the Henry E. Huntington Library, San Marino, California.

1

Social Context

Perhaps more than any other writer of his generation, Jack London was profoundly affected by his environment and his time. "Born only fourteen years before the 1890 census marked the closing of the Frontier, coming of age during that decade called the watershed of American history, and dying less than a year before the United States entered World War I, London personified the most crucial transition in this nation's cultural development."[1] With one foot in the past and the other in the future, London noisily straddled the two centuries as easily as he straddled three of the major social classes in the United States: the lower class, the underworld, and the upper-middle class. Last of the writers to celebrate the American Frontier and first to trumpet the battles on the frontier of social justice,[2] he was truly the voice of a transitional period: loud, positive, vigorous, and extremely controversial. His thinking and his work were influenced by the conflicting social forces of industrialism and capitalism on the one hand and of socialism on the other, as well as by the social and racial theories of his time.

The process of industrialization begun before the Civil War reached its full force by the end of the nineteenth century, when the

United States actually led the world in the production of such commodities as coal, iron, and steel, and changed the way of life of the American people. Rural dwellers and immigrants were forced to move to the cities in order to find jobs. Urban areas developed tremendously, and the poverty of the workers in New York and other large cities equaled, if not surpassed, that of European workers, as vividly dramatized by Upton Sinclair's *The Jungle*.[3] The capitalistic system, which was based on laissez-faire and individualism, was unstable and moved through uncontrolled cycles of prosperity and recession. The panic of 1893 was one of the worst recessions in American history: the value of the dollar fell, banks closed, railroads went into receivership, commercial firms failed, and thousands were unemployed. With the panic came increased demands for workers' protection and security, and in 1894 Jack London took part in a mass protest when he joined the West Coast contingent of Coxey's Industrial Army, led by Charles T. Kelly ("Kelly's Army"), on its march from the West Coast to Washington, D.C., to complain against economic conditions.

Because of his lower-class upbringing, London was familiar with the problems of the poor. For years he had been a "work-beast" until he revolted and decided to get out of the working class at all cost. While his adolescence had been devoted to Horatio Alger's belief that honesty and hard work would be rewarded, he became rather disenchanted after a few stints as a manual worker in the industrial shop: a cannery for 14 or more hours a day when he was 15, a jute mill when he was 17, an electrical power plant where he shoveled coal when he was 18, unknowingly doing as a scab the job of two men for a salary of $30 a month (lower by $10 than the salary of one regular employee), and finally a laundry in 1897 when he was 21—his pay still being $30 a month. He left the Belmont Academy laundry determined not to return to the treadmill of the working class, and, years later, he vividly dramatized his three months of exhausting laundry work in *Martin Eden*.

Added to the horror of the poverty he had witnessed in the East End of London, which he recalled in *Martin Eden* but dramatized in naturalistic fashion in *The People of the Abyss*, these experiences made him deeply sympathetic to the rise of socialistic ideas. Socialism, which erupted in Europe around the midnineteenth century, reached

America toward the end of it. The labor movement emerged out of the workers' feelings of helplessness and powerlessness, and the Workingmen's Party of the United States was established in 1877, soon becoming the Socialist Labor Party. In 1896 Jack London joined the American section of the Socialist Labor Party in Oakland. The socialist movement grew through the 1880s and 1890s, and various parties emerged with their own philosophies on how to fix the world. Right-wing parties called for parliamentary reforms, while more radical parties insisted that only class revolution could cure society's ills. Predictably, London was a radical who eventually resigned from the party in 1916 because of its antiwar stance. He had, however, withdrawn from active involvement in the party much earlier out of disappointment with the mediocrity of its leaders and the conviction that it would go nowhere since Americans prefer democratic to revolutionary methods.[4] He also felt he could reach more people through his work than through political action and devoted his considerable energies to his writing and to the developing and improving of his ranch, becoming one of the first dedicated environmentalists.

London's experiences in the underworld also helped shape his thinking and made him all the more aware of man's cruelty and of the necessity of being a survivor. When he was 15, London borrowed money to buy a skiff (the *Razzle-Dazzle*), joined a gang, and began robbing the oyster beds of legitimate fishermen in San Francisco Bay, netting $25 for one night's work, almost as much as he made in a month of grueling labor in the cannery. London's turning to oyster piracy and entering a criminal subculture was a characteristic response of urban lower-class youth but also evidenced his budding rejection of the world of the poor. London slipped further into the underworld when he began his tramping career after leaving Kelly's Army of the Unemployed, but, paradoxically, he saw this experience as a sort of apprenticeship for his literary career: "The successful hobo must be an artist. He must create spontaneously and instantaneously—and not upon a theme selected from the plenitude of his own imagination, but upon the theme he reads in the face of the person who opens the door. . . . I have often thought that to this training of my tramp days is due much of my success as a story-writer."[5]

However, his tramping days ended unpleasantly between the bars of Erie County Penitentiary where he was locked up on a vagrancy charge. There he learned fear and humility, and not to stand up for his rights when the odds were against him. One might interestingly parallel the breaking of Buck by the man in the red sweater in *The Call of the Wild* with the beating of the young mulatto in *The Road*, London's record of his experience as a tramp, which concludes: "It is not a nice thing to see a man's heart broken in a minute and a half" (*Road*, 108–9).

Many of London's age were caught between two worlds as new political and economic structures forced a change in their old way of life and values, and the past came to represent with nostalgic regret a simpler and more innocent life. Thus, when George Washington Carmack discovered gold in 1896, the Klondike was hailed as the Last Frontier, and thousands of dissatisfied Americans sought wealth and refuge in the Yukon. When the news of Bonanza River reached the United States in 1897, it was met with unprecedented madness. Approximately 250,000 gold miners started out during the two big years of the rush, only 50,000 of whom reached the interior, and fewer than one-seventh found any gold. According to Franklin Walker, "The Klondike rush was, in fact, as insane a gamble for fortune, as perverse a movement toward the wilderness to escape a crowded world, as that world has known to date,"[6] and, according to Earle Labor, it was the logical outcome of the social and spiritual situation in the United States:

> The mood of unquiet desperation in America's response may also be understood, if not justified, by the times. The United States was still recovering from the worst depression of its history. The swelling of American cities after the Civil War; the spreading stain of poverty and slums; the suffocating railroad tariffs which imposed on the Western farmers all the traffic would bear; the squeezing out of the small independent businessman by the giant monopolies; the political corruption of "The Great Barbecue"; the moral hypocrisies and social affectations of the genteel mode—in short, revulsion against all the decadence of the Gilded

Age galvanized by the nation's yearning to recapture its lost youth. (*Jack*, 36)

London was immediately captivated by the promise of the Gold Rush and was among the first Americans to leave. He had grown up in the San Francisco area, "the heart of America's most spectacular Frontier," and was naturally inclined toward adventure. Indeed, he would always try to escape the drabness and monotony of life through adventure, and he saw the Frontier and the return to nature it implied as a means of escape from the horrors of modern life and as a place where courage, endurance, and intelligence, not a bank balance, determined the status of men. He left on 25 July 1897, and, if he brought back no gold from the Klondike, he brought back experiences and a vision he readily turned into gold afterward.

The last important social force shaping London's thinking seems to have been his entrance into the middle class when he became a successful writer. London saw his rejection of the lower class and his entrance into the intellectual middle class as both a progression and a regression. He saw it in terms of a choice between a masculine world of raw power and a more feminine world of culture, literature, and bourgeois hypocrisy. Such a transition could not be made smoothly, and he never could relinquish entirely the world of "men." Indeed, London must have found it very difficult to go back to high school after having been self-sufficient for many years, a sailor before the mast and a tramp. Small wonder that after two years of studying, he should have joined the Gold Rush enthusiastically.

The "civilizing" of Jack London climaxed in his hurried marriage to Bessie Maddern, with whom he was not in love. His spur-of-the-moment proposal was largely motivated by an abstract desire to settle down and by the feeling that he would work better and be a better man for it. Not surprisingly, because of their complete incompatibility of character, he found the yoke of domesticity galling and expressed it in terms of his previous experiences. The life of a sailor on the sea or of a worker in a factory comes down to breaking others or being broken. In marriage, however, he felt that his hands were tied, that he could only bow his neck: "to be broken while not daring to break, there's the rub."[7] London could never reconcile the two worlds, and he became as contemptuous of the squeamishness and hypocrisy of the intellectual middle class as of the brutality of the lower classes and underworld. He yearned both for intellectual stimulation and for the ability of the sailor to live intensely and enjoy the simple beauties of life. A loveless marriage did not help reconcile such opposites, and he remembered with nostalgia the years when he was free, when there were no constraints and he did what he wanted. London saw the two ways of life as incompatible and irreconcilable, unless perhaps by marriage to a "mate-woman" who could share his yearning for adventure and follow him wherever he went. He found that woman in his second wife, Charmian Kittredge.

These opposite tendencies, which pulled at him throughout his life, are vividly dramatized in *Martin Eden*. But, while Martin eventually commits suicide because he feels unable to resolve the conflict between a middle class he despises and the world of raw power he can no longer belong to or enjoy, London kept trying to reconcile the two in his life and in his work. When he succeeded, as in *The Call of the Wild*, he opened up worlds of forgotten and all-consuming emotions. Unlike Martin, Buck, under his beautiful coat of fur, can choose the world of violence, survival, and freedom, and live in it unhampered by literary or ethical considerations.

Among the books that most influenced London's social thinking were Marx's *Das Kapital*, Henry George's *Progress and Poverty*, and Herbert Spencer's *Principles of Sociology*, *Principles of Psychology*, and *First Principles*, which he had already read by 1896. He took Charles Darwin's *On the Origin of Species* (and John Milton's *Paradise Lost*) to the Klondike. He had also read Thomas Huxley by 1897, to which he would add Henry Drummond, John Fiske, Herbert Conn, and Josiah Strong by 1900. His social reading in 1901 included in particular Ernest Haeckel's *The Riddle of the Universe* and Emile Vandervelde's *Collectivism and Industrial Evolution*. Throughout his life, London kept reading extensively to document his sociological studies. For instance, while he was hard at work on *The Call of the Wild*, he was reading Jacob Riis's *The Battle with the Slum*, which he would use for his essay "The American Abyss," and Enrico Ferri's *Criminal Sociology*, which prompted the beginning of a file on criminals that would in turn provide material for *The Star Rover*. In fact, he never stopped reading the sociological studies published in his time.[8]

London was impressed by Darwin's evolutionary ideas and the concept of the survival of the fittest, making social Darwinism the basis of his personal philosophy. Darwin, Huxley, and Spencer became the "bedrock of his thought and writing, underlying even the socialism which was his faith."[9] London was also captivated by the late-nineteenth-century application of evolutionary theories to race. Benjamin Kidd's *Social Evolution* (1894) "applied the principle of natural selection to society, only to conclude that the mass of men must consent, in the interest of progress, to yield to a few superior individuals who will be selected to rule society and to keep it at the maximum of its efficiency." The evolutionary ideas suffusing the philosophy of Friedrich Nietzsche also held sway over London. As early as his Yukon days, London was beginning to be conscious of a personal ideal that later, after exposure to Nietzsche, would dominate his work. "He visioned a certain type of white man who could equal the physical prowess of the finest specimens of primitive man, and outdo them, as well as his less favored white brothers, in intellectual power and achievement" (*Times*, 143).

London was fascinated by abstract concepts and by the clash between conflicting concepts, which he repeatedly dramatized in his work, thus often leading critics to conclude that he was philosophically confused. Whether one sees this as intellectual confusion or as the manifestation of a remarkable imagination and wide powers of identification is up to the reader's personal bias. If one takes individually any one of London's stories at face value, one will be led to conclude that he is at once a racist, a Nietzschean, a fascist, a humanist, an animal lover, an animal hater, a socialist, an elitist, a spiritualist, a materialist. But if one considers his work at large, one cannot but conclude that he was a man exploring the human fact in all its aspects, both beautiful and ugly, as objectively as he could.

Jack London was thus very much a child of his time whose mind absorbed new concepts and translated them in fictional terms. Because he was open to many different and often conflicting ideas, critics have found it difficult to reduce him to one overriding vision of life and have thus concluded that he was a minor writer. However, London's fantastic and enduring world fame and the stature of *The Call of the Wild* as a world classic suggest that North American literary critics should take a much closer look at his work.

2

Literary Influences

London's discovery of the world of books was as instrumental as his social milieu in shaping his vision of life. He was a voracious reader from his earliest years until his death, by which time he owned more than 15,000 books, most of which he had read and many of which he had annotated. Moreover, until he could afford to buy books in large numbers, he was a devoted customer of lending libraries. After having discovered his first book—Ouida's *Signa*—when he was eight, he took his first steps in a library of any size in 1886 when his family moved to Oakland, and he considered this one of the most wonderful things that had happened to him: "Not until I began fighting for a living and making my first successes so that I was able to buy books for myself did I . . . discontinue drawing many books on many library cards from out of the Oakland free public library."[1] According to his childhood friend Frank Atherton, Jack read an average of two books a week. Later, in *John Barleycorn*, London described his youthful passion for books: "I . . . was reading myself into nervous prostration. . . . I read everything, but principally history and adventure, and all the old travels and voyages. I read mornings, afternoons and nights. I read in bed, I read at table, I read as I walked to and from school, and I read at recess while the other boys were playing."[2] London's vast reading included not only sociological, scientific, and ethical studies, but also literature and psychology, including American and European classics as well as the works of contemporary novelists. Later in life, he discovered with delight Freud's theories of the subconscious and Carl Jung's theories of racial memory and the collective unconscious—concepts he had repeatedly and instinctively dramatized throughout his work.

By 1900, London's literary readings included in particular a medley of Charles Dickens, Sir Walter Scott, Rudyard Kipling, Robert Louis Stevenson, William Shakespeare, Henry Wadsworth Longfellow, Robert Browning, Alfred Lord Tennyson, Ambrose Bierce, John Keats, Frank Norris, Stephen Crane, Harriet Beecher Stowe, William Makepeace Thackeray, Thomas Carlyle, Oscar Wilde, Joseph Conrad, Arthur Schopenhauer, Mark Twain, John Ruskin, Bret Harte, Edgar Allan Poe, Edmond Rostand, Paul Bourget, Victor Hugo, Jean-Jacques Rousseau, and many others.[3] Rudyard Kipling, to whom he paid repeated tribute, was perhaps the single greatest literary influence on his early work. But he soon became interested in the Realists and Naturalists, both French and American, and he was always a charitable reviewer of his own contemporaries, such as Frank Norris and Upton Sinclair who, like him, were exploring in their novels the social reality of their time.

That London was familiar with the literary schools of French Realism and Naturalism is clear. In his personal library, he owned books by Honoré de Balzac (25 volumes), Guy de Maupassant, and Gustave Flaubert, and 22 of Emile Zola's novels, with dates of publication ranging as far back as the 1880s, including, in particular, the 1903 edition of *Truth* between the pages of which he had written on a small card: "Remember me when this you read." It seems that he was reading Zola's *Germinal* as early as his oyster-pirating days on the sloop *Reindeer*, and he mentions Zola both in *A Son of the Sun* and in *Mutiny on the Elsinore*.[4] Whether he was familiar with *The Experimental Novel*, which was available, having been translated into English in 1893, is unknown because he does not seem to mention it anywhere. However, he certainly did abide by the basic rules set out by

Zola for writing naturalistic fiction, and his vision of what fiction should do coincided closely with Zola's.

Emile Zola was in fact a major influence on late-nineteenth-century American writers such as Stephen Crane, Frank Norris, Hamlin Garland, William Dean Howells, and Theodore Dreiser. Indeed, interest in contemporary French literature was a striking feature of the cultural life in the United States during the last decade of the nineteenth century: "Just now we are trying to be French, yesterday we were cultivating the Russians; last week the English had us under their thumbs."[5] However, Naturalism was not to everybody's taste, as voiced by Thomas Bailey Aldrich's poem "At the Funeral of a Minor Poet":

> The mighty Zolaistic Movement now
> Engrosses us—a miasmatic breath
> Blown from the slums. We paint life as it is,
> The hideous side of it, with careful pains,
> Making a god of the dull Commonplace.[6]

Nevertheless Zola was extraordinarily popular in the United States, as evidenced by the numerous translations of his work. Between 1878, the date of the first English translation of one of his novels, *Une page d'amour*, and 1900, 31 American publishers brought out approximately 180 books by Zola. "For twenty-one years every eight months some new publisher entered the market with one or more books from the pen of Zola, and eight times a year, during this period, a new American translation of Zola was put on sale,"[7] and the sales were "unprecedented." Indeed, as may well be added proof of Zola's popularity, novels he had not written were published under his name: one bearing the title of *Emile Zola's First Love Story* and published by Jewett and Buchanan (Chicago) in 1895, and the other titled *The Two Duchesses*, published in New York by F. Tousey's *Brookside Library* in 1884.

The translations of the novels and their titles suggests an obvious appeal to sensationalism on the part of American publishers, which would have angered Zola. In fact, he was indignant at the self-righteous moralistic criticism which had been leveled against his work, referring to it as "the mass of rubbish that had been heaped upon [him],"[8] and he always kept his titles very terse to avoid any form of sensationalism. However, American publishers exploited the deep-rooted Puritan idea that the literature of France is essentially wicked and transformed Zola's plain and direct titles into popular-romance titles: *la Fortune des Rougon* was translated as *The Rougon-Macquart Family*, but also as *The Girl in Scarlet* and *Wedded in Death*; *Une page d'amour* became *Hélène: A Love Episode*, *A Woman's Heart*, and, worse, *A Stray Leaf from the Book of Love*; *la Conquête de Plassans* became with increasing bad taste *A Mad Love*, *The Abbé and His Court*, *A Fatal Conquest*, or *Buried in the Ashes of a Ruined Home*; *Madeleine Férat* was translated as *Driven to Her Doom* and *The Finger of Fate*; and *Thérèse Raquin* became *Nemesis* and *Haunted by the Specter of a Murdered Man*.[9]

American publishers who would never have published anything that came close to Zola's novels in frankness by an American author, as evidenced by the fate of *Sister Carrie* in 1900, made the most of the opportunity Zola afforded. American readers could thus read novels that dramatized life in all its aspects, including what was to date the frankest portrayal of sex, while still feeling secure that such things happened only in France and that, in America, all men were honest, altruistic, and faithful to one and only one woman, to whom they were married; that no one lived in dismal poverty and vice; that women were either wives or prostitutes, and that the prostitutes were few in number and soon to be redeemed by society; and that people did not murder one another for sex or money. Indeed, to publicize Zola's work, American publishers capitalized on the very thing Zola despised most and fought against throughout his career.

Like many of his contemporaries, such as Gustave Flaubert, Zola started out as a Romantic, being particularly fond of the works of Lamartine, Victor Hugo, and Alfred de Musset, and having a general dislike for the Realists. However, working at Hachette's, he met many of them and eventually changed his mind. While he still criticized the Realists' approach to literature, feeling that one cannot touch dirt without dirtying one's hands, he began to concede that they probably gave the most accurate picture of reality. Believing that any literary school is monstrous in that it makes nature lie according to a set of rules, he elaborated his own theory of colored lenses: in any work of art, the reader is made to see the world through the eyes of the author's temperament and personality, likes and dislikes, fears and dreams, which act as a screen between the world perceived and its dramatization. Thus the reality portrayed cannot be accurate, since it will change with every new screen. Similarly, lenses of different shades color differently the objects seen through them, while concave and convex lenses change the shape of these same objects. Perfectly aware that no work of art could ever be completely objective in its portrayal of reality, Zola concluded that, despite the inherent limitations of the human mind and eye, Realism offered the best chance to portray reality objectively, since the screen of Realism willed itself to be so transparent as virtually to negate its own existence. To use Stephen Crane's words, "a man is born into the world with his own pair of eyes and he is not at all responsible for his vision—he is merely responsible for his quality of personal honesty." Crane was proud that men of sense believed him to be sincere, and he felt that this was the only goal worth striving for, although a man was sure to fail at it.[10]

Zola was particularly influenced by Claude Bernard's *Introduction à l'étude de la médecine expérimentale.* Already familiar with Darwin's *On the Origin of Species*, Lucas's *Traité de l'hérédité naturelle*, as well as Spencer's *First Principles*, Zola saw Bernard's application of the experimental method to the study of the human body as a model for the possible study of the human mind and of society, explaining his premise in *le Roman expérimental* (*The Experimental Novel*, 1880). Postulating that, since any phenomenon taking place in a living being is determined, Zola concluded that the human mind is itself determined by strict laws: "Un même déterminisme doit régir la pierre des chemins et le cerveau de l'homme." Society, composed as it is of individuals who are controlled by their milieu and heredity, must have its own laws that can in turn be ascertained and studied. The experimental novel must then do for the cerebral and sensual activities of man what medicine did for the human body. In the manner of a scientist, the experimental novelist must make use of all the knowledge compiled by other sciences in his investigation into the nature of man and of society, following the same steps (observation, hypothesis, and experimentation), hazarding a hypothesis only insofar as it respects all the facts that are known, and using intuition only with regard to facts that have not yet been proven. With this aim in mind, Zola based the naturalistic novel on a set of five basic rules which can be summed up by the following key words: *accuracy*, *noninvolvement*, *amorality*, *rejection of social taboos*, and *determinism*.

The naturalistic novel must be a documentary novel based solidly on physical reality and crammed with facts and data actually seen and experienced. Reality, hard and brutal as it might be, must be described with an exact minuteness of detail. The novelist must collect human documents through careful preparation and endless toil. A hard worker whose slogan was "Travaillez, tout est là," Zola thoroughly researched the topics he dramatized. The 20-novel series of the "Rougon-Macquart" gives an accurate picture of French society under the Second Empire, dealing with the social and economic questions crucial to that time and ranging over the various social strata. In fact, Zola compiled an enormous amount of documentation and had files on most things. When he was working on *Germinal*, a novel dramatizing the life of coal miners, he spent time in Enzin in 1884, during a major strike, lived with the miners, went into the mine, studied the conditions of their work, went into their houses, and did not leave until he felt he had a good grasp of the situation. Zola thus gave in his novels a well-documented and accurate picture of his time.

The attitude of the naturalistic writer toward his material must be one of utter noninvolvement, abstaining from positive or negative comments, presenting facts objectively, never showing his own personality or turning to the reader for sympathy. The naturalistic novel should neither preach nor satirize but only dramatize human life objectively and draw no conclusions, as the conclusions are implicit in the material. Zola wanted the naturalistic novel to be a powerful social tool, but he felt that an accurate and objective picture of society and mankind presented with clinical detachment was more effective than a compassionate dramatization of man's misery. A classic illustration of this type of writing is the death scene in Flaubert's *Madame Bovary*.

Dramatized with scientific detachment, Emma Bovary's agony from arsenic poisoning is described in purely clinical terms.

Closely linked to the noninvolvement credo is Zola's belief that morality is no more relevant to art and literature than to science. Thus, moral implications have no place in the naturalistic novel, which should never condemn its characters for their actions. The naturalistic novel is therefore "amoral" in the sense that it recognizes no relevance to morality. Not surprisingly, the Naturalists were damned as "immoral," in particular because of their frank portrayal of sex. It is partly as a response to such attacks that Zola wrote *The Experimental Novel* and *The Experimental Novelists*, which offer a formal explanation of theories he had already put into practice in his work, since, by 1880, he had already published eight of the twenty-book series of the Rougon-Macquart. Indeed, because it is to provide a frank portrayal of all aspects of human life, the naturalistic novel cannot shun subjects until then considered taboo, such as prostitution, free love, social misery, and the burning questions of the day. Because they dealt with such topics and exposed without mercy the ugly aspects of life, the Naturalists were accused of having a predilection for the ugly details of modern civilization; but this aspect of their art has been overstressed: not all their books deal with the slums, neither do they all deal with physically weak or mentally impaired people. However, for the first time, the lower classes became heroes and heroines of grim tales, a new subject matter that was treated with a sincerity and brutality unknown before. The frank portrayal of sex was particularly characteristic of French Naturalism, love being reduced to sexual desire and depicted as a physical craving, such as hunger and thirst, and as a natural force that struck blindly its victims. This approach agreed with the importance given to man's instincts, the relative denial of free will, and the inability to control natural urges. *Thérèse Raquin* (1868), a novel that does not belong to the Rougon-Macquart series, offers perhaps the most striking portrayal of love as an irresistible physical force.

Finally, Zola believed that, just as animals are transformed by the surroundings in which they live and to which they have to adapt in order to survive, human beings are fashioned by their environment. He felt that man cannot be separated from his milieu; that his clothing, his house, his city, his province are all part of him, and that everything taking place in his heart or in his mind is motivated by his milieu and in turn affects that same milieu. The whole purpose of the Rougon-Macquart series is to show how a family, a small group of people, behaves in society and gives birth to 10 or 20 individuals who, at first glance, are very different but who, in the final analysis, are intimately linked one to the other. Zola intended to find and follow the thread that led "mathematically" from one man to the other, while solving the double equation of temperaments and the influence of the milieu.

While Zola based the Rougon-Macquart series on the double hereditary factor of madness and alcoholism, he gave equal importance to the influence of the milieu and expanded the study of character to embrace the entire physical man, his physical impulses and instincts. Using copious documentation, facts of modern scientific civilization, and strictly accurate details of urban, industrial, or rural life, Zola did not content himself with a cold demonstration but turned it into great poetry and created a world of symbols and overpowering atmosphere, of intense emotions and desires, of people who are struggling blindly to achieve a measure of happiness in a world animated by oppressive and often malignant powers.

It is easy to find fault with Zola's theory, for its weaknesses are obvious to us now. He thought that the discoveries of science were sufficient to explain man through the laws of heredity and evolution and that one could experiment with man as with things. Clearly, man is far too complex a life-form to be studied as a metal or a chemical product; the theories of heredity and evolution were not fixed in Zola's time, nor are they fully explored even now. Moreover, fiction could never become a science, as Zola believed, for no experimentation is possible in the writing of a novel where the author largely controls his material. However, one should remember that in Zola's time, the discoveries of science had been tremendous in almost every field of human knowledge, and one might well say that in no other period of human history did mankind make such extraordinary advances in the knowledge of the world, its origins, its inhabitants, and the forces that control it. It is therefore hardly surprising that people began to believe that science had the answer to everything, and that it could account for the universe, for thinking man, and for God himself. Indeed, Zola was modern in that he tried to apply the discoveries of his time, and saw that a new understanding of man could be brought about by these discoveries. If he was perhaps naive and too rigid in his application of these new theories, he nevertheless opened new fields of investigation and introduced ideas and facts to the novel that were valid and explained aspects of man that had hitherto remained mysteries or belonged to the world of myth.

Sigmund Freud, whom London began reading in 1912, and Carl Jung, whom he discovered in 1916, clearly could not have influenced as early a work as *The Call of the Wild*. However, they fascinated him because he found in their theories a formal explanation of concepts he had sensed and struggled with instinctively and dramatized throughout his work. His study of Carl Jung's *Psychology of the Unconscious* in 1916, the last year of his life, might have influenced his writing more than any other, had he had more time left. His passionate interest in the book is mirrored by the inordinate number of annotations he made in it: in no other book in his library did he make as many as 300. As it is, during the last six months of his life, he wrote a half-dozen remarkable stories incorporating Hawaiian mythology with Jung's theories of archetypes and the collective unconscious, among which a masterpiece, "The Red One"—a treasure trove of archetypal riches and at the same time a prophetic work, anticipating such stories as both Arthur C. Clarke's *The Sentinel* and *2001* and foreshadowing the horrors of Auschwitz and Hiroshima.[11] When London remarked that *The Call of the Wild* had been "a lucky shot in the dark" (*Times*, 252), he was more accurate than he could possibly have known and had unknowingly expressed the mythical appeal that has made the book a unique world classic. Jack expressed his fascination for Jung in revealing terms when he said to Charmian: "I tell you I am standing on the edge of a world so new, so wonderful that I am almost afraid to look over into it."[12] If "The Red One" consciously dramatized archetypal themes and motifs, *The Call of the Wild*, *Before Adam*, and many of his earlier novels and stories did so unconsciously, but no less effectively.

19

3

The Importance of *The Call of the Wild*

The Call of the Wild is unique in its appeal to readers of all ages, social classes, and civilizations. Since its publication in 1903, it has been the most widely read American novel in the world, and its fame is far from diminishing. It holds the attention of everyone—men and women, boys and girls, the uneducated as well as philosophers and scholars.

Like Saint-Exupéry's *le Petit Prince*, it is a fascinating animal story loved by children, with a lovely, big dog as the hero. A child will cry and laugh over it, pore over maps of Alaska to find the real places, and dream of wonderful adventures in the frozen North. But, as an animal story, it stands apart from the others and, in many ways, can be considered the epic of the dog and of the wild land it dramatizes.

It is also an exhilarating tale of adventure where ancient passions rage—the struggle for survival, the blind courage, the triumph and glory of victory that have not yet died in the heart of man. Men and women who live on the vestiges of Frontiers that have all but disappeared, pent up in cities and tied to the machines of our modern age, find in London's work at large a refreshingly primitive and elemental life and live vicariously the lives of heroes, whether prospecting for gold in Alaska, sailing the Northern Seas with *The Sea-Wolf*, adventuring in the islands of the South Pacific, or venturing on the seas of scientific or social speculation. *The Call of the Wild* dramatizes vividly London's belief in the return to the elemental, to what is fundamental in man and nature, to the strength born of struggle, and to the age-old spirit of adventure.

Intellectually inclined readers find in *The Call of the Wild* a brilliant human allegory of the buried impulses and of the descent into the depth of both the unconscious and a primordial past shared by men and beasts alike at the dawn of humanity. While the protagonist is a dog, the buried impulses belong as much to mankind as to the animal world, and London's use of a fur-coated hero allows him to say much more about the human situation than would otherwise have been allowed by contemporary readers and editors, or even by modern readers. It allows him to cut through human pretenses, squeamishness, and hypocrisies to get to the heart of the matter and dramatize the *self striving for psychic integration* and the process of *individuation*. Unlike Kurtz, Buck finds no unbearable horror in this *Heart of Darkness*, and through him the reader can learn to accept and even exult, if only for a moment, in his own primordial self without having to relinquish the advantages of civilization.

Part adventure-romance and part human allegory, the book is also a naturalistic document on Klondike life during the Gold Rush as well as a gripping tale of devolution. As a result of a sudden change in social and living conditions, Buck, a tame and pampered dog, must learn the skills of survival, dig into his primordial past, and find in himself the inheritance of his wild forebears as a condition for survival. Again, London's choice of a canine protagonist allows him to explore the stages of devolution unhindered by the moral barriers a human protagonist would have entailed and to present us with a virtual anatomy of devolution that we can readily accept.

The Call of the Wild is also a mythical book informed throughout with such traditional myths as the Myth of the Hero. The stages of the myth are all present—the call to adventure, departure, initiation, the dangerous journey into the "world's navel," transformation, and apotheosis—but the journey does not end in self-destruction or isolation, as is so often the case with human heroes. Instead, it ends with social and racial integration, with Buck's assuming almost godlike attributes.

Emotionally, psychologically, mythically, and archetypally satisfying, *The Call of the Wild* is also ethically and romantically satisfying. London's essentially positive vision of life and his own dreams of freedom pervade the novel. Love is the most powerful animating force in the story: the love of work and of physical exertion, the love of man, and, above all, a passionate love of life. The protagonists actualize themselves fully. There are no lukewarm emotions or compromises in this book's dramatization of a simple and basic struggle; and the working out of natural forces is essentially just, both transcending and integrating the harshness of the naturalistic vision. There is nothing absurd in this book where humans make their own hell, and where almost everything can be explained in terms of natural causes and effects. Beauty as well as love and justice pervade the book: the beauty of Buck, which London emphasizes time and again, but also the beauty of the White Silence and of London's often inspired prose. London captures the romance of the North, and his descriptions transform this frozen immensity into a psychological dimension, a dazzling and pitiless entity with the fascination of eternity. One might say that London has captured the soul of the North and has created its God in Buck. As the tale progresses and as Buck becomes one with his self and with nature, London's prose becomes increasingly lyrical and reaches pitches of remarkable beauty. By the last chapter, we have a prose poem, a hymn to life and survival, to the integrated self, and to the passions that lift one out of the mundane.

In *The Call of the Wild* London creates a world that is vibrantly alive, celebrating life, freedom, and the joy of being. He goes beyond the superficial niceties of life to touch the roots of life, the primordial emotions that are firmly seated in all men and were the dominant emotions of the primitive world. In it London captures the essential meaning of life and the basic human being through Buck who has all the attributes of an ideal hero: gorgeous, powerful, wild, free, and pure. Is it any surprise that the world has been, and still is, enthralled by this novel?

4

International Critical Reception

London began writing *The Call of the Wild,* the book that would one day make him famous, as a 4,000-word companion to an earlier dog story, "Bâtard." However, within a two-month span (1 December 1902 through January 1903), London had completed a 27,000-word novel. As he explained in a letter to his editor, George P. Brett, "The whole history of this story has been very rapid. On my return from England I sat down to write it into a 4,000 word yarn, but it got away from me & I was forced to expand it to its present length."[1] Macmillan snapped up the rights to the book for $2,000 cash, and the American serial rights were sold to the *Saturday Evening Post* for 3¢ a word, bringing in an additional $750, which London received on 3 March. This was probably the worst deal London made in his life, for the copyrights alone for this book, which sold by the ten millions of copies around the world, would have solved many of the financial problems that plagued his life. But he had really no idea that he had written a world's best-seller and classic, and he merely expected that Macmillan would get a "fair sale" out of it. He had originally turned down Macmillan's offer on 9 March, believing that his having already disposed of the serial rights to the *Saturday Evening Post* and to Watt and Son for the English serial sale had "knocked in the head" Macmillan's plans for publishing the book, but he changed his mind when he found out differently and accepted it on 25 March, signing his contract on 2 April. The success of the novel was immediate, and all 10,000 copies published in July 1903 sold out on the day of publication. Between 1903 and 1947, 6 million copies of *The Call of the Wild* were sold in the United States.

Shortly after its publication, the book was very favorably reviewed. Arthur Bartlett Maurice, for instance, reviewed it as "far and away the best book that Mr. London has ever written" in the *Bookman* of October 1903, while the reviewer for the *Athenaeum* described it as "the best thing the public has had so far from the pen of a young author who, though he made his first bow but yesterday, has already shown a fresh and vigorous bent in story, combined with a certain amount of originality and dramatic power."[2] *Current Literature*, after deeming the book London's best "piece of work," added that the novel "rises above the mere storytelling, and possesses elements of the best in literature—scope, vitality and fullness,"[3] and William Morton Payne overcame initial reservations about the basic premise of the book to write in *The Dial*: "Mr. Jack London has certainly done a clever and appealing piece of work in *The Call of the Wild* which must rank high among animal stories . . . [and] is sufficiently convincing to dull skepticism while it is being read. Doubts arise afterwards, and they are probably legitimate, but while the spell of the story is upon us, we are willing to allow that a dog may have the complex inner life which is here depicted."[4]

Most reviewers were quick to praise London's novel as an allegory of the human condition, despite the fact that London himself, although aware that the book was utterly different in subject and treatment from the average animal story, denied having consciously written it as an allegory. Kate B. Stille argued that "the telling thing in the book is its underlying truth. The call of the wild is no fiction. The things pointed out are the nameless things we feel, and the author shows clearly, unobtrusively . . . that man and dog are mastered by the wolf cry, striving after things alive."[5] However, the reviewer for the *Atlantic Monthly* felt that, although a deeper meaning can be found in the novel, it is most enjoyable as a simple animal and adventure story: "*The Call of the Wild* is a story altogether untouched by bookishness. A bookish writer might, beginning with the title, have called it An Instance of Atavism, or A Reversion to Type. A bookish reader might conceivably read it as a sort of allegory with a broad human application; but its face value as a single minded study of animal nature really seems to be sufficiently considerable."[6]

Apart from the reviewers who liked the book but did not grasp its greatness, were those who hated it and those who immediately realized that they had read a great work of literature. The reviewer from the *Charleston News* was clearly upset by it. Granting that it had generally been received with a chorus of praise and that it was considered "one of the best things of its kind in English literature," he nevertheless found the novel particularly disagreeable:

> We do not dispute its power, its dramatic force, its picturesque character, and (with certain limitations) its psychological quality. But it is, for all that, a brutal, repulsive picture. Nine-tenths of the book absolutely reeks with cruelty. There are pages upon pages which no one with ordinary sensibility can read without acute pain and vehement indignation—the indignation which comes from the spectacle of tortures inflicted by savage men upon animals far more noble than themselves. . . .
>
> On the whole "The Call of the Wild" may be frankly admitted to be a vivid and picturesque tale, but if it is "a piece of literature" we are very much mistaken.[7]

Based on personal prejudice rather than on an educated or open-minded understanding of an art form, this shortsighted and bigoted review ironically grants London's novel the very qualities that make it a great work of literature while damning it for reasons that have nothing to do with its artistic value: its topic.

Others, such as Mary Holland Kinkaid, instinctively grasped the importance of the work and its greatness. Sensing its archetypal appeal, she saw it as "one of the imperishable tales which belong to the whole world." "Balzac's 'A Passion in the Desert' is numbered among the greatest stories that men have told to one another, but it suffers when compared to this latest work of the California author who for the last three years has been proving that he is the inheritance of genius. . . . Mr. London has told his story with the simplicity which is the highest mark of literary excellence."[8] The reviewer for the *Louisville Courier Journal* also sensed the book's directness and simplicity and stressed its deeper appeal—"Humanity answers the deep cry of this tale. A great undercurrent is carried below the surface of the story, a force old as the world, the cry of a younger world which the dog loved to sing."[9]—while George Hamlin Fitch recognized London's "complete mastery of his material and that unconscious molding of style to thought which marks real from make-believe literature."[10]

Indeed, *The Call of the Wild* has been a continued source of reading enjoyment for a vast and varied readership, as well as a source of interest to critics. To a large extent, recent analyses of the novel examine its allegorical implications. Both Earl J. Wilcox and Roderick Nash attribute the popularity of the novel to its allegorical dimension: "The book is allegory; it deals with dogs but pertains to men. In describing Buck's progress from tameness to wildness, the author passed judgement on his contemporaries. They too, he implied, suffered from overcivilization, and in the early 1900's the idea struck a sympathetic chord."[11] Although most critics have viewed Buck's movement as a progressive development, a few have interpreted it as a negative movement, with John Perry notably arguing that "Instead of evolving according to the progressivism of Herbert Spencer and Benjamin Kidd, Buck regresses both morally and socially."[12] Both Earle Labor and Joan Hedrick analyze *The Call of the Wild* in terms of the Myth of the Hero, seeing Buck's quest as evolving from the civilized and familiar to the primitive and natural, ultimately reaching the supernatural. Through his North-bound travels into the primitive, Buck becomes a furry incarnation of the archetypal romantic quest figure, makes a perilous journey into the "world navel" or mysterious life center, where he undergoes transformation and finally apotheosis. Moreover, Labor parallels Buck's spiritual development with the stylistic development perceivable in the novel, showing how the quick, fierce rhythms of the early chapters gradually give way to an increasingly lyrical style.[13]

Others, such as Raymond Benoit, view Buck's journey in terms of the pastoral motif, with Buck moving from an essentially corrupt and impotent civilized world into a simpler, more honest existence. Like Huckleberry Finn, Buck becomes the embodiment of the American Dream of escaping from the increasing complexity of the modern age into an earlier time, blissfully unencumbered by the entanglements of civilization.[14]

Other interpretations of the novel emphasize its autobiographical content. Pierre Berton saw it as a classic largely because it is based to a large degree on London's experience piloting boats on the Whitehorse Rapids during the Gold Rush, while Joan London observed the similarities between Buck's and her father's experiences: both London and Buck left their domestic surroundings, however unwillingly on Buck's part, and found adventure in the North; both rose from poverty or underdog status to a position of distinction and authority, Buck as lead sled-dog and leader of the wolf pack and London as a leading American author.[15] More recently, Andrew Flink argued that Buck's experiences closely parallel two crucial events in London's life: the unqualified rejection of London by his natural father and the time when London was arrested for vagrancy in Niagara Falls and sentenced to 30 days in the Erie County Penitentiary. Flink bases his comparison on the facts that Buck and London are both strong, healthy, and approximately the same age (London was 18, and Buck approximately 20, if one counts one year of a dog's life as the equivalent of 5 years of a man's); Buck was sold to pay a gambling debt with which he had no connection, and London was arrested because of a debt he felt he had never incurred; both Buck and London are forcibly transported and confined, and neither are ever able to forget this traumatic experience.[16]

Finally, there are the strangely enduring examinations of London's work in the context of his socialist beliefs. While some of London's other works, such as *The Iron Heel* or *Martin Eden*, lend themselves readily to such an ideological interpretation, even the most enthusiastic critic has difficulty making a convincing case for an interpretation of *The Call of the Wild* in this light. Joan London, for instance, describes Buck's journey as a flight from the unbearable reality of the struggle for existence in a capitalist society to a clean, beautiful, primitive world in which the strong can survive, while Carolyn Johnston feels that Buck represents the Nietzschean superman in animal form and "demonstrates comradeship based on love and solidarity against environmental forces."[17]

While the novel was generally well received in London's native country, this critical reception appears meager when compared with the enormous recognition it has enjoyed abroad. As of 1975, book-length translations of London's works had been published in 68 languages; currently his work appears in 86 languages and is constantly reedited throughout the world, being particularly popular in Russia, South America, Poland, Sweden, France, Germany, and China.[18] For instance, between 1975 and 1985, no fewer than 14 new or reprinted translations of London's works appeared in Bulgarian, 11 in Dutch, 60 in French, 117 in German, 16 in Bulgarian, 38 in Italian, 64 in Russian, and 68 in Spanish. Some countries, such as France and Germany, have in fact much more of London's work in print than the United States.[19]

Introduced in the former Soviet Union shortly after the revolution in 1905, London's works found a widespread, early, and enduringly loyal reading audience. London has been the most popular American writer in Russia until recently, when he started sharing first place with Ernest Hemingway. More than 13 million copies of his works have been printed in Russia since the revolution, and during World War II London's works were singled out for publication when other American writers were consciously ignored.

> No other foreign writer published in our country has [had] such a great circulation as Jack London, and this is not accidental. The spirit of manliness and struggle, the spirit of disinterested friendship, run through all of his works. . . . Faith in man and in his limitless strength and possibilities conquered millions of human hearts for the famous American writer. We have kept the works

of Jack London in singular pre-eminence amongst our translated literature—17 million copies of his books have been published in our country. No library, even a small household one, can do with[out] the romantic and grim . . . works of London. His stories were loved by V. I. Lenin. A. M. Gorky regarded London as the originator of proletarian literature in America.[20]

Surprisingly, London's popularity in Russia cannot be attributed to the socialistic sentiment pervading much of his work. Deming Brown attributes London's appeal to the vigor of his writing, his hearty temperament, and his love of violence and brute force and feels that the Russian taste for stories of hardy adventure in remote and uncivilized territories was cultivated largely through London's works.[21] Lenin's widow wrote that two days before his death Lenin had asked her to read aloud to him "Love of Life": "It was a very fine story. In a wilderness of ice, where no human being had set foot, a sick man, dying of hunger, is making for the harbour of a big river. His strength is giving out, he cannot walk but keeps slipping, and beside him there slides a wolf—also dying of hunger. There is a fight between them: the man wins. Half dead, half demented, he reaches his goal. That tale greatly pleased Ilyich."[22]

Paradoxically, the socialistic overtones of many of London's works were partly the cause of a brief but notable ebb in his popularity in Russia in the late 1920s, largely as a result of the publication in 1927 of a Russian translation of an article by Joseph Freeman condemning London for preaching socialism while leading a materialistic life. Thus, a contradiction was perceived between his "word and deed," which the Russians found difficult to accept. However, this was a short-lived cooling of their appreciation, and they soon returned to reading and enjoying their favorite American novelist.

Since 1925 London's works have also drawn large and varied reading audiences in Mexico, Central America, and especially South America. In addition to several other London works, *The Call of the Wild*, a clear favorite in Spanish America, was translated anew and published in Spanish no fewer than four times between 1935 and 1975: *O grito da selva*, translated by Monteiro Labato (1935); *A voz da selva* by

Luisa Maria de Eca Leal (no date); *O apelo da selva* by Emilia Maria Bagao e Silva (1963); and *Chamado selvagem* by Sylvio Monteiro (1967 and 1972).[23] Arnold Chapman attributes London's popularity in Spanish America to the widespread distribution of Hollywood movies dramatizing adventures in the frozen North, and in particular Charles Chaplin's *The Gold Rush*. Chile, in particular, as the last land conquered by the Spaniards and an active participant in the Gold Rush, had many reasons to sympathize with its northern neighbor.[24]

A lesser known, though considerable, readership of London's works can be found in Poland, where London is by far the most popular and widely read American writer. Between 1945 and 1965 no fewer than 81 works of London's were published in Poland, and between 1955 and 1965 London had more works published in Poland than any other writer. However, even at the peak of their popularity among a general reading audience, London's works did not receive extensive critical coverage.[25] Similarly, in Sweden, London's works amassed an early, sizable, and tenacious reading audience among the public, while remaining to a large extent ignored by scholars and critics.

The first of London's books to be published in Swedish was *The Call of the Wild* in 1907. By 1957 five collected editions of London's works were available in Sweden: a 32-volume edition published between 1917 and 1922, a 20-volume edition published in 1927, two 15-volume editions published in 1929, and a 16-volume edition published in 1939.[26] A 1951 survey of circulation in Swedish lending libraries revealed London to be the most popular American author, a popularity attributed by Carl Anderson less to London's socialist views than to the intense spirit of adventure pervading his work and the simplicity and directness of his style.

In France, London's work continues to be well received by a general reading audience and is also discussed at length in literary circles. Such a warm critical reception did London's fiction receive between 1905, when the first translation of one of his works appeared, and the beginning of World War II that 32 translations and 19 separate reeditions of London's works followed. The first critical analysis of London's fiction appeared in 1908, shortly after its first translation, and between 1908 and 1939, 20 reviews and five critical essays on

London's work appeared in France. Jean Gonnet, the first French reviewer of a London novel focused on *The Call of the Wild*, praising its realism and comparing it with the works of H. G. Wells. Gonnet commended London's directness and concision in presenting amazing facts and felt that the novel was a "neat evocation of a milieu totally new." Régis Michaud similarly wrote later that London excels at dislocating the civilized and "at rejuvenating them upon contact with the primitive."[27] Mary Sue Schriber attributes London's appeal in early-twentieth-century France, where American literature was still viewed as vulgar and mercantile Colonial English literature, to a love among the French for the bizarre and the unusual. Not that there is much that is bizarre in London's work, but, like Edgar Allan Poe, he captured the French imagination better than other American writers largely because of the universal, romantic, and allegorical quality of his work. His naturalism was also a genre with which the French were familiar and of which they were deeply appreciative. Schriber also points to the French fascination with London's life of adventure and suggests that in France London became the archetype of the self-made man making the difficult climb from extreme poverty to success, and a larger-than-life symbol of the American Dream.

Although the Germans were rather slow in appreciating London's work, they quickly closed the gap with other European countries. London felt for a long time that he would never be popular in that country, in particular since German publishers had a habit of picking and choosing from his work rather than publishing whole books. He sarcastically recapitulated the situation as it had been presented to him by Robert Lutz, a German publisher, in October 1909: "The German public cares very little for my work. The best way to get the German public interested in my work is to get them to read some of my work. According to your judgement, the way to get the German public to read some of my work is to spoil two of my books by taking several stories from each of them and publishing them in German."[28] Clearly London's private opinion of the publishing world in Germany was not very flattering. Moreover, since they paid few royalties, he had little interest in having anything to do with the German market. By 1914, however, to use his own words, he was having a "mild vogue" in Germany, and he felt that it was time to bring the German publishers, Lutz in particular, to their knees: "The Germans have proved always to be a cheap bunch in the matter of translation rights; and if we fail in this our attitude we have little to lose; and if we succeed, we make the bunch come to us and take our stand in the matter. . . . Now is the time, if such be so, to make the German publishers come to our terms; and our terms are primarily that no collection of short stories be broken up in the manner that every last one of the cream-skimming German publishers suggest."[29] Despite this inauspicious beginning in London's relationship with German publishers, an appreciation of London's writing rose quite early in Germany, beginning with the publication of *The Call of the Wild* in 1907 (and again in 1912 and 1916), followed by *Burning Daylight* (1911), *White Fang* (1912), *When God Laughs* (1912), *The Sea-Wolf* (1912), *South Sea Tales* (1913), *Martin Eden* (1913), *A Son of the Sun* (1913), *The Son of the Wolf* (1913), and *Before Adam* (1915). After 1918 no fewer than 70 editions of London's works were in print in Germany. Although noteworthy by 1918, London's reputation in Germany increased dramatically when the Universitas Verlag in Berlin took up his books in 1924 and published a long series of translations through the interwar period, eventually bringing out London's *Collected Works* in 1940, a year during which most other American authors were ignored in Germany.

Anne M. Springer's excellent examination of London's critical reception in Germany between World Wars I and II attributes London's popularity in pre–World War II Germany to several factors. No other American author appealed as wholeheartedly to the diversified tastes of the postrevolution German reading public of the 1920s, and London came to be associated with the energetic forces of a new world overtaking a tired, war-worn nation. London was "like a fresh breeze from another world, a healthy robust man of sweat and toil." London's "unknown energy and lust for life" appeared to one critic as a "relief from the thousand psychological probings and tortures which the European romancer prepares for him." Springer also suggests that many admired the fact that London did not become aligned with the early-twentieth-century German "literati." According to F. M.

Reifferscheidt, "The reader all over Europe [had] become sick and tired of the problems and spiritual ills of the literati—[was] it any wonder that London's descriptions based on experience seem[ed] wholesome and excellent." Another reason for London's popularity was the Germans' fascinated discovery of his life through Charmian London's biography, which was translated into German shortly after its publication in the United States. London's popularity in Germany may also be attributed in part to his predilection for Nietszche's concept of the superman and the superwoman.[30]

Translations of London's works began appearing in China in the late 1920s. It seems that the cultural giant of modern China, Lu Xun, first read *The Call of the Wild* in Japanese[31] and was so impressed that he determined to introduce London's works in China because he felt that "they [were] just the right thing for present-day China." *The Iron Heel*, "The Dream of Debs," and "The Apostate" were published in 1929 in Shanghai, the largest Chinese cultural center at the time, and *The Iron Heel* became so popular that it had to be reprinted the following year. The Commercial Press and Books of China published a translation of *The Call of the Wild* six years later in its world classics series at the same time as another major publisher brought out its own translation of the novel together with "A Piece of Steak" and "The Chinago." The novel went into reprint in 1938 at a time when China was at war. *Martin Eden* (1943, 1947), *White Fang* (1947, 1948), and three volumes of short stories followed. By 1949, most of London's novels and some of his best stories had Chinese translations. A new surge of interest in London's work became manifest in the early 1950s, and during the 1950s and 1960s, when China was completely cut off from the West, London, Mark Twain, and Theodore Dreiser were the only modern American writers known and accessible to the common Chinese reader. London also occupied a conspicuous position in literary courses for students of the humanities. A few critical studies of his work also appeared in the late 1950s, most of the scholars considering him an outstanding American Realist and some calling him the founder of proletarian literature in America.[32] In the 1970s London studies took on new momentum but began to recede in the 1980s when the cultural exchanges between China and the United States became more active, which may well be the result of the influence of American critics. For instance, a 1984 article entitled "Early Naturalistic Literature of the U.S."[33] was clearly influenced by Charles Walcutt's chapter on London in *American Literary Naturalism: A Divided Stream*. However, Chinese readers continue to enjoy London's work, and students still choose to write their theses on his work.

Indeed, London's world fame far outranks his fame in his native country. Paradoxically, while he is considered a major world writer, he is not yet considered a major American writer, and he is reluctantly included, if at all, in anthologies of American literature. Just as Edgar Allan Poe's immense popularity in France as a result of Charles Baudelaire's brilliant translations forced American critics to reconsider his work, London's enduring popularity worldwide is now prompting a serious reassessment of his literary achievement, and London probably will eventually be granted the place that should be his in American literature.

A READING

5

A Dream of Freedom

Jack London began writing *The Call of the Wild* on 1 December 1902, shortly after his return from England. The years 1902 and 1903 were difficult and confusing ones for him, involving a growing dissatisfaction with his marriage to Bessie, an increasing restlessness, the end of a love affair with Anna Strunsky, and a two-month immersion in the East End slums of London, England (7 August–30 September). The short stay in the West End of London and the continental vacation following it were not enough to allow him to recover from the trauma created by the intense and overwhelming mass of misery to which he had been privy. Consciously or not, writing *The Call of the Wild* allowed him to indulge in a revivifying and cleansing dream of freedom from the shackles of personal duty in a passionless environment, and in a dramatization of a vibrant and natural world of beauty and rationality as an antidote to the horrors of the human jungle he had discovered.

London's marriage to Bessie was a failure. In his own words, they were not mated; they were uncongenial, and they were not happy.[1] He was increasingly of the opinion that, as a "poor human," he had the right to seek "a bit of happiness in compensation for the pain of living." Although he had not yet fallen in love with Charmian Kittredge, he was acutely aware that passion was lacking in his life and that his wife was in no way the companion he had dreamed of—a mate who would be so much one with him that she could never misunderstand, who would love the flesh as well as the spirit, honoring and loving each and giving each its due, whose personality would include both fact and fancy, practical with regard to the mechanics of life and fanciful, imaginative, sentimental with regard to the thrill of life; a mate who would be delicate and tender, brave and game; sensitive in soul, unfearing and unwitting of pain in body; warm with the glow of great adventure, unafraid of the harshnesses of life and its evils, and knowing all its harshness and evil.[2] Charmian would later come to embody this ideal mate and companion, but, in the meantime, Bessie was its exact opposite. By 1902, their relationship had become a tug of war. She refused to take part in his sports and games, enjoying neither swimming, fencing, boxing, nor horsing around on the beach. She was sexually cold, refused to play charming hostess to the "Crowd," the Bay Area bohemian intellectuals he had befriended, or to dress in an attractive and feminine fashion as befitted her role as wife of a successful writer. She was possessive, manipulative, and preoccupied with gossip, proclaiming from the rooftops every wrong she had, felt she had, or invented she had suffered at Jack's hands, and she was suspicious of every woman who came into contact with him, going through his wastebasket and piecing together torn letters to substantiate her suspicions. She was intellectually as well as emotionally dishonest, and Jack would later describe her as "one of the most colossal and shameless liars [he had] ever encountered."[3] London summarized his mood in the latter part of 1902 and the early part of 1903 as follows: "I was not in a very happy state. You will remember, yourself, the black moods that used to come upon me at that time, and the black philosophy that I worked out at that time, and afterwards put into Wolf Larsen's mouth. My marriage was eminently unsatisfactory. . . . I had made up my mind to go to pieces and get a separation. This without being in love with anybody, but from sheer disgust in life, such as I was living it."[4] He felt for a long time that he was "bound in a miserable chain of circumstances, which [he] was too selfish to break—both from fear of hurting [himself], and of hurting others which would likewise have been hurt to [him]."[5] Bessie's dislike of physical intimacy sent London out with George Sterling in search of adventures, his all-night prowls leaving her terrified that he would bring back some venereal disease. Sterling even made his house available for Jack's private meetings with Blanche Partington, a music and drama critic, who competed with Charmian Kittredge for his affections in 1904.

An unconventional man, London wanted a wife who could share his fun and adventures, who was sensual and tender, comfortable in a crowd of friends and happy to be alone with him for weeks at a time, courageous and daring, athletic and feminine. He had little interest in the traditional type of wife, wholly devoted to children and house-keeping. Although he wanted children and a comfortable home life, he wanted his wife to be above all a "mate." His 1910 inscription in Charmian's copy of *The Road* clearly evidences his expectations: "Dearest My Woman: Whose efficient hands I love—the hands that have worked for me long hours and many, swiftly and deftly, and beautifully in the making of music; the hands that have steered the Snark through wild passages and rough seas, that do not tremble on a trigger, that are sure and strong on the reins of a thoroughbred or an untamed Marquesan stallion; the hands that are sweet with love as they pass through my hair, firm with comradeship as they grip mine, and that soothe as only they of all hands in the world can soothe."[6] There was no double standard for London, and he dramatized his ideal conception of womanhood early in his work. Strong, honest, self-reliant, passionately devoted women abound in his early stories of the North. They are often Indian women, but not always, and London respected personal qualities wherever he found them, irrespective of race and gender. In fact, his female protagonists are often stronger than his male characters, and he often dramatized the tragedy of a strong, passionate, and self-sacrificing woman married to a weaker, self-indulgent man with less integrity.

London dramatized, probably subconsciously, the ideal partnership he dreamed of in Buck's relationship with John Thornton. In the love that links them, both Buck and Thornton retain their dignity and integrity, Buck never seeking out tokens of affection as do the other dogs. They roughhouse but never hurt each other. "Buck had a trick of love expression that was akin to hurt. He would often seize Thornton's hand in his mouth and close so fiercely that the flesh bore the impress of his teeth for some time afterward. And as Buck understood the oaths to be love words, so the man understood this feigned bite for a caress" (109). Man and dog are totally devoted to each other and worthy of the other's love: Buck is willing to give his life for that of Thornton time and again, and Thornton accepts Buck's need for freedom in the woods and never tries to curtail it. When they travel, they are partners rather than dog and master, each strong, self-reliant, and able to survive in the wilderness without the other's help.

London's sensuality also comes through in his descriptions of Buck. His constant emphasis on Buck's beautiful, silky, furry coat reminds one of his love for furs, silk, lace, fineries, jewelry, and precious stones. After Bessie's frustrating dislike of such pleasure-giving articles, London discovered with delight Charmian's "inordinate fondness for pretty things"[7] and indulged her and himself fully. Their marriage, which remained a passionate affair until the end, turned out to be, among many other things, a cheerful and enthusiastic shopping spree for beautiful things, which Charmian faithfully recorded in her personal diaries. Buck's glorying in his physical self and in the hunt, in the play of each muscle and sinew, also mirrors London's delight in the physical, his pride in pushing his body to its limits, and his enjoyment of strong sensations in contact with nature. London's sensuality was sorely thwarted by his marriage to Bessie but found expression in his descriptions of Buck and of Wolf Larsen in *The Sea-Wolf*, emphasizing in each case visual and tactile appeal. London's relationship with Charmian, which began in June 1903, would also satisfy this aspect of his personality, and he would discover with infinite pleasure that her sensuality equaled his, that she enjoyed sports, such as swimming and horseback riding, that she was an habituée of body and facial massages, that she kept herself fit and beautifully dressed, and that she appreciated beauty as much as he did.

Buck's life until his meeting with John Thornton mirrors London's life until his affair with Charmian Kittredge in its lack of passion for another being. London had known several infatuations and love affairs, none of which had been very satisfactory. He had known women early, claiming that he had a consort during his oyster-pirating days, and he remained a familiar visitor to brothels and engaged in short-term sexual involvements before and during his marriage to Bessie:

> As passionate as you [Cloudesley Johns] with probably less curb, I think I must have been created for some polygamous country. While I have a strong will, I deliberately withhold it when it happens to clash with desire. I simply refuse to draw the curb. When I was just sixteen I broke loose and went off on my own hook. Took unto myself a mistress of the same age, lived a year of wildest risk in which I made more money in one week than I do in a year now, and then to escape the inevitable downward drift, broke away from everything and went to sea.[8]

His first love for Mabel Applegarth, "a delicate, golden-haired, blue-eyed dainty,"[9] whom he vividly dramatized in *Martin Eden* as Ruth Morse, was unfulfilling. While he idealized her for a time, he outgrew his infatuation with the realization that she was a conventional and unadventurous *petite bourgeoise*, but he remained friendly with her for the rest of his life. His marriage to Bessie was motivated neither by love nor by desire but by the mistaken idea that it would help him settle down: "Sunday morning, last, I had not the slightest intention of doing what I am going to do. I came down and looked over the house I was to move into—that fathered the thought. . . . Sunday evening I opened transactions for a wife; by Monday evening had the affair well under way; and next Saturday morning I shall marry—a Bessie Maddern. . . ."[10] He was honest with Bessie, though, and made it quite clear that he did not love her when he proposed, an absence of feelings she apparently shared. In 1900 London also seems to have held the notion that marriage and love were largely a biological phenomenon rather than an emotional one—an issue he discussed at length with Anna Strunsky in an exchange of letters published in 1903 as *The Kempton-Wace Letters* in which she argued that love should be a basis for intimacy and marriage.

When he proposed to Bessie, London was probably already attracted to Anna, whom he had met in the fall of 1899. She struck him as a beautiful and rebellious genius who made Mabel Applegarth look like a pale and superficial mannequin. His need to justify his marriage to Bessie to her is revealing: "For a thousand reasons I think myself justified in making this marriage. It will not, however, interfere much with my old life or my life as I planned it for the future."[11] Again, he was mistaken as he would soon come to recognize. The work on *The Kempton-Wace Letters* brought Jack and Anna closer together, and by the spring of 1902 he was "sick with love for [her] and need of [her]."[12] Anna idealized Jack but would not give herself to him, although she worked closely with him, occasionally staying in his house while they were proofreading the *Letters*. The relationship changed while London was in England, and Anna discovered that Bessie was expecting another child. Furious, she wrote to him, accusing him of having lied to her; he replied just as angrily, contemptuously pointing out that she knew nothing about things sexual: "Work back nine months. Come ahead again to the time at the Bungalow when we held speech upon a very kindred subject. Bearing these two periods in mind, if you have any superficial knowledge of things sexual and physiological, you will fail to discover any lie. If you have not this knowledge, & I do not think you have, consult some woman who has."[13] He concluded: "the Sahib is dead, and forgiven as the dead are forgiven. Poor devil of a Sahib! He should have been all soft or all hard; as it is, he makes a mess of his life and of other lives." This was the end of their love, but not of their friendship.

Bitter about his marriage and about Anna's lack of understanding, London spent a winter of unhappiness and self-doubt, sitting down to writing *The Call of the Wild* shortly after his return from Europe and transcending his frustrations in the story of Buck who, after much traveling and suffering, eventually finds love—"love that [is] feverish and burning, that [is] adoration, that [is] madness" (108). But even for Buck, this love has to end when Thornton is taken from him, mirroring London's doubts that he would ever know a love that was strong and passionate enough to last his whole life. Ironically, London did find the kind of passion he had so vividly dramatized in the novel a few months after completing it. In June 1903 he sent Bessie and the children off to camp at Glen Ellen and began looking for a sailing companion for a few days. He wanted a mistress, and his thoughts turned to Charmian among others, who seemed to be "a warm enough proposition to suit [him] in an illicit way."[14] To his own surprise, her honesty, frankness, and lack of "coy flutter" won him over immediately, and he was in love after one night. This love, despite an inauspicious first few months, while they had to battle the Crowd, Bessie, and even Jack's other affair with Blanche Partington, lasted until his death.

London's plunge in the East End of London, which immediately preceded the writing of *The Call of the Wild*, was a traumatic experience. He saw more misery and suffering there than he had ever dreamed could exist despite his own rough initiation into the world of adulthood. Expressions of horror recur in his letters of the time: "The whole thing, all the co[nd]itions of life, the in[t]ensity of it, eve[ry]thing is overwhelming. I never conceived such a mass of misery in the world before." "I am made sick by this human hell-hole called London Town. I find it almost impossible to believe that some of the horrible things I have seen are really so."[15] London thought he had seen much suffering during his years in the Californian underworld and the industrial sweatshop, but it was nothing by comparison with the chronic starvation and filth which was the lot of the East Enders. The squalor of the living conditions he had witnessed and experienced for a few weeks shocked him immensely, but what he found even more unbearable were the consequences of the unrelieved deprivation of all that is basic to human life and dignity on the East Enders: "I have seen men's eyes here, & women's, that I was almost afraid to look in—not because of the viciousness ther[e]in, nor the sensuality, or anything of the sort, but because of the utter lack of all these, because of the supreme bestiality or unhumanness. I should not like to be God. Nor, if there be a God, should I like to be a West-Ender."[16] It is thus hardly surprising that London felt compelled to write a book dramatizing the need for a return to nature after this brutal vision of an urban jungle and of the human beings who lived in it in various states of degradation, starvation, and misery, bullied, mistreated, and ignored by the higher levels of society. Indeed, he felt that a man was better off in the American wilderness, where he could retain his dignity, never lacking clothing, fuel, and housing and only starving occasionally, than in the East End of London, where one perpetually lacks these essentials. His conclusion at the end of *The People of the Abyss* is clear: "There can be no mistake. Civilization has increased man's producing power an hundred fold, and through mismanagement the men of Civilization live worse than the beasts, and have less to eat and wear and protect them from the elements than the savage Innuit in a frigid climate who lives today as he lived in the stone age ten thousand years ago."[17]

Mismanagement, indifference, and incompetence are always at the root of much suffering in London's work, and, in *The Call of the Wild*, the only unbearable and useless suffering is inflicted by the trio of incompetent *chekakos*. The way Hal, Charles, and Mercedes manage the dogs upon whose work and survival depends the success of their expedition and their own survival in the frozen wilderness parallels the way the manpower in the East End of London is managed: callously, stupidly, wastefully, inefficiently, and counterproductively. London indirectly vented his anger at the gross and criminal mismanagement he had witnessed in the East End in his portrayal of these incompetent dog drivers, and their fate foreshadows the fate London envisioned for the British Empire and for the industrial world at large.

But, in general, if dogs and men suffer in *The Call of the Wild*, it is an episodic suffering relieved by moments of joy and sheer pleasure in the physical work they perform. London had no objection to hard work, even grueling work, provided it served a purpose and was managed efficiently, as the professional drivers manage their team, whether they are François and Perrault, the "Scotch half-breed," or Thornton and his friends: "Each night the dogs were attended to first. They ate before the drivers ate, and no man sought his sleeping-robe till he had seen to the feet of the dogs he drove" (87). The miniature society formed by the dogs and their drivers is neither sentimental nor soft, but it is coherent and efficient and might well serve in London's opinion as a model for human society. As one who "loved his fellow-men and wanted to make life better and nobler for all,"[18] London could not abide the appalling waste of the capitalistic system as epitomized by the East End, which transformed the poor into "twisted monstrosities . . . inconceivable types of sodden ugliness, the wrecks of society, the perambulating carcasses, the living deaths—women blasted by disease and drink . . . and men, in fantastic rags, wrenched by hardship and exposure out of all semblance of men, their faces in a perpetual writhe of pain, grinning idiotically, shambling like apes, dying with every step they took and each breath they drew."[19] He could not believe either in the eventual success of a socialist movement, which he felt was led by mediocre leaders whose theories had little contact with reality and "who trusted to the Marxian forecast of economic, political and mental development."[20] He found that the mass of humanity was still mentally mediocre and ill informed and believed that the only way to improve it was to place its fate in the hands of a superior type of humans which neither the capitalists nor the socialists could claim to represent. London's lack of hope for the betterment of mankind is vividly dramatized in one of his science-fiction stories, "Goliah." In it, London envisions enforced happiness and peace among mankind by a scientific superman and world tyrant, master of ultimate power, who creates, by force, a society based on intelligence and compassion. The message is clear: only under the threat of slaughter will mankind accept happiness and work toward it. By contrast with existing society, the dog teams in *The Call of the Wild* offer a rational form of cooperation when dog drivers and lead dogs are competent, with the best of them in the lead. However, even the most brilliant lead dog can do nothing to avert disaster when the humans holding the whip are idiotic and self-indulgent.

Writing the novel thus afforded London an opportunity to transcend his personal, emotional, and intellectual disappointments. It also allowed him to lose himself in a world of beauty and purity, which contrasted sharply with the repulsive world of filth and deterioration he had discovered in England. Despite its literal and symbolic coldness, despite its awesome power and immensity, despite its lack of forgiveness for errors and weaknesses, the White Silence, the vast, still, and frozen Northland wilderness, is a symbol of freedom and purity. While the minds and bodies of survivors rot slowly in the putrid slums, the White Silence provides a moral and physical school of endurance over which presides a harsh but just God. If the weak die quickly in the North, the survivors become stronger and better adapted to an environment which intensifies the life force in them. They live close to nature; they experience its bounty and beauty; and they pit their will to live against the dangers of a land frozen under its pall of snow, with "the aurora borealis flaming coldly overhead, or the stars leaping in the frost dance" (74). While the North provides no warmth or security and thus does not offer man a satisfactory version of Paradise, its coherence may foster a certain serenity and pride in men who have returned to a simpler life. For creatures which have returned to the wild like Buck, it offers the ultimate satisfaction of perfect harmony with basic instincts and the surrounding wilderness.

6

A Tale of Devolution

"No man who sojourned in the Northland during that time of the early argonauts but admits an obligation to you. Wherever men of the Yukon foregather your name is spoken, for you have voiced for us the things we saw and felt and can put into words but vaguely. No one else has done it. . . . I have read all your books . . . [and] sometimes when I read, there comes to me a great yearning for the untrod stretches of the far land. Occasionally I see in your descriptions a familiar face or an unforgotten scene. Here is a man with whom I slept in the snow; that is a creek which I prospected; here is an incident with which I am familiar and which seemed but commonplace to me until touched by the wand of genius."

Thus wrote W. B. Hartgrave to Jack London on 2 March 1913, praising the Klondike tales which "tell of the great river and the long trails; of hardship and hunger; of the howl of the wolf dog; of the silent nights and the blazing sky."[1] This was high praise for a realistic writer who strove to recreate the way it was in his works. London was indeed devoted to the premise of realistic and naturalistic fiction, and his vision of what fiction should achieve was similar to Emile Zola's.

London took the gathering of documentary evidence very seriously, and he would go to great lengths, such as getting himself imprisoned, to gather data for a story. For instance, wanting to write an American version of his own *The People of the Abyss*, he intended to find "some hell-hole of a prison, and have [himself] arrested and sent to it."[2] When he was researching *The People of the Abyss*, he lived for seven weeks the life of the poorest among the workers and vagrants who lived in the East End of London. He slept and ate in sordid hellholes where people had to wait in line for six or more hours before being admitted, where bunks were slept in continually in shifts of eight hours, and where one had to break 1,200 pounds of stone or empty the garbage of hospitals and be exposed to contagious diseases such as typhoid for the privilege of sleeping in a filthy bed for one night. He saw the ugliest aspects of death and the most miserable ones, such as the death of an old woman who used to make candies for a living and stored them in the very room where her son was dying of tuberculosis. After seven weeks of such a life, London emerged from the East End scarred, but with a well-documented and violent indictment of a society that allows men to be reduced to a level of existence below that of the animals.

Before undertaking a new story, London would also carefully research his subject, collecting newspaper clippings, articles, magazines, and books filed according to topic for ready reference. He kept files for future use on every topic that might be of interest. For instance, he accumulated over 15 years a file containing 28 newspaper articles on prison life, which he used when writing *The Star Rover*, thereby supplementing Ed Morrell's personal memories of San Quentin with other factual data. One of these articles, "Red Shirt Men of San Quentin," published in the 7 May 1899 *Sunday Examiner Magazine*, 15 years before London actually wrote *The Star Rover*, deals with convicts who tried to escape and who are afterward compelled to wear crimson, becoming plain targets for the guards. Six men had to wear these red shirts, among them Ed Morrell who had been sentenced to life imprisonment and who, after he was pardoned, asked London to write the book as part of a campaign to have his friend Jake Oppenheimer reprieved.

Although at times London's fiction moves into science fiction and astral projection, it is firmly grounded in reality. However fantastic some of his stories may appear, they usually satisfy the requirements of logic and known scientific data and are based on human documents, such as the "little death" sections of *The Star Rover*, which deal with astral projection.

London firmly believed in evolution and determinism, and the influence of heredity and the milieu, as evidenced by much of his work and abundant notes. He saw these concepts as basic facts of life over which man has no control: "The different families of man must yield to law . . . to LAW, inexorable, blind, unreasoning law, which has no knowledge of good or ill, right or wrong; which has no preference, grants no favors, whether to the atoms in a molecule of water or to any of the units in our whole sidereal system; which is unconscious, abstract, just as is Time, Space, Matter, Motion;—This is the law, the higher logic, which the petty worms of men must bow to, whether they will or no."[3] Countless of his story outlines evidence the fact that he intended to dramatize the influence of heredity and the environment, such as the following: "Write a book in two parts—*Part 1*— begin with father & mother & develop the heredity, all the potencies of the boy. Then a healthful environment that realizes the good potencies, defeats the bad ones, or even makes the bad ones powerful for good. *Part 2*—take same basis, same father & mother, same baby, and bad environment (remember Orloff & his wife) & work out a different life."[4]

London had been too influenced by his reading of Darwin, Spencer, and Auguste Comte not to be a confirmed determinist and evolutionist; but these beliefs are tempered by a deep love of humanity, by a loathing for the cold-blooded, deliberate cruelty that often characterizes man's treatment of animals and other men. London's accurate descriptions of the inhumanity of man are not a gloating over blood and knuckles, as so many critics have believed, but an expression of his abhorrence of cruelty and of his belief that the best way to expose it is to describe it unemotionally and accurately.

Indeed, London believed that the writer must eliminate himself from his story and not express his own feelings concerning what he is describing. In a vibrant defense of Kipling's methods and of the apparent heartlessness of his descriptions, London makes his point clear: "And what more is the function of art than to excite states of consciousness complementary to the thing portrayed? The color of tragedy is red. Must the artist also paint the watery tears and wan-faced grief?"[5] He felt that objectiveness in the description of horror was far more effective than any expression of sympathy or pity, as he indicates in his review of Maxim Gorky's *Foma Gordyéeff*. "One lays the book down sick at heart—sick for life with all its 'lyings and its lusts.' But it is a healthy book. So fearful is its portrayal of social disease, so ruthless its stripping of the painted charm from vice, that its tendency cannot but be strongly for good. It is a goad, to prick sleeping human consciences awake and drive them into the battle for humanity."[6]

This was also Zola's eventual aim: show life as it is, so that people will do something to improve it. Not that a writer can ever really show life as it is in a book, as most of the Realists were acutely aware of, for the truth is not always believable, and fiction is what seems real, not what is real. London himself was often infuriated when readers refused to believe in the reality of characters he had modeled on real people he had known and concluded ruefully: "one cannot do on the printed page what one does in life."[7] Love and sex, however, were Truths London found hard to handle in a naturalistic fashion because he well knew that American readers would not accept a frank portrayal of love from an American writer. Indeed, "He followed Truth only up to the portals of the boudoir; behind those doors Truth remained veiled" (*Comrade*, 79). While London suggests passionate love in many of his stories and novels, he never describes it as such, and it only manifests itself in its results: the extent of what the lover is willing to do for the loved one. But physical contact he never describes in any detail between human beings.

Except with regard to the frank portrayal of sex, London was thus very much in tune with the requirements of naturalistic fiction as established by Zola. In fact, very much like Zola, London was a hard worker who believed in the necessity of working all the time. Echoing Zola's "Travaillez, tout est là," his advice to literary aspirants was:

"WORK, WORK all the time. . . . Don't loaf and invite inspiration: light out after it with a club, and if you don't get it you will nonetheless get something that looks remarkably like it."[8] As a result of such dedication, both men left a remarkable body of work (more than 50 books for London, and some 40 books for Zola), among which are some of the world's great classics.

Although not directly dramatizing the social problems of the day, since its main protagonist is, after all, covered with a thick coat of fur, *The Call of the Wild* is in many ways a naturalistic novel that gives an interesting dramatization of Klondike types, as embodied by the four different sets of masters who in turn own Buck: the essentially just and efficient François and Perrault (the government couriers), the "Scotch half-breed" who is in charge of the mail train, and the other drivers who are also just, despite harsh circumstances, and who respect the dogs and spare them what suffering they can. The last two sets of masters Buck works under are dramatically opposite: first are the self-indulgent, lazy, and hypocritical Hal, Charles, and Mercedes, who are stupid, greedy, ignorant, have no respect for the dogs, and are made to stand for the worst of the *chekakos*; second is John Thornton, the ideal master, "[who] saw to the welfare of his [dogs] as if they were his own children, because he could not help it" (108). Clearly, London could not dramatize through the eyes of a dog many characteristics of the social reality of the Klondike of the 1897 Gold Rush, but he could and did make what human characters he portrayed widely representative of the Klondike types he knew and had heard of—types one finds repeatedly in his other stories of the North.

London's documentation was fairly extensive, since he spent nearly a year taking part in the Gold Rush, leaving San Francisco on 25 July 1897 on the *SS Umatilla*, disembarking at Juneau, and eventually rafting down the Yukon, scurvy-ridden, the following spring. London's party made the trip from Dyea Beach to the Stewart River, where they decided to settle for the winter in two months, arriving on 9 October, four days before the river traditionally froze, and taking possession of a cabin on an island between the mouth of the Stewart River and the mouth of Henderson Creek. Jack toiled mightily with the rest, daily increasing the load he was packing, until he was proud to be able to pack as well as the Indians, carrying 100 pounds to the load on good trails and 75 pounds on bad ones. Since he had 1,000 pounds in his outfit, he took every load for one mile and came back for the next, thus walking 19 miles for every mile of progression if he carried 10 loads and 29 miles if he carried 15 loads.[9] Their route took them over the Chilkoot Pass to Lake Linderman, where they constructed a boat (9–21 September). Jack's skill in handling small boats stood them in good stead, and they made their way through lakes Linderman, Bennet, Tagish, and Marsh before entering Fifty Mile River which narrowed into two dangerous rapids: Box Canyon and White Horse Rapids. They ran the rapids safely but encountered a storm at Lake Laberge, which delayed them for three days. The river trip from Lake Linderman took them a little less than three weeks, and they decided to make camp on Upper Island, between the Stewart River and Henderson Creek, which seemed to be a wise choice since Dawson would be crowded and there was the threat of food shortage. Moreover, they could travel to Dawson easily once the Yukon had frozen, and they could do a little winter mining if they found a promising area.

They staked eight claims by 16 October and made their way downriver by boat to Dawson, where London spent six weeks, during which he had ample opportunity to get impressions of the gold city. Dawson woke to find the Yukon frozen on 5 November, the same day London filed his claim at the gold-records office for his gold strike on Henderson Creek, 18 days after arriving in the city. London spent a great deal of time in Dawson's saloons, often in conversation with some veteran sourdough or noted Dawson character. It was also in these bars that sourdoughs were famous for gambling away their fortunes. If *The Call of the Wild* dramatizes only two scenes in a saloon—the scene at Circle City in which Buck attacks "Black" Burton, and the scene in the Eldorado Saloon in Dawson as a result of which Buck is made to pull a sled with 1,000 pounds of flour—many of London's stories of the North dramatize the aspects of life in Dawson he had witnessed, the drinking, talking, gambling, dancing, and the places, saloons, restaurants, Opera House, and commercial stores he had frequented. The only aspect of life in Dawson he avoids describing is prostitution, which was rampant; this, of course, is very unnaturalistic, but the reasons for the omission are obvious. In fact, dance-hall girls are always treated kindly and gallantly in London's Klondike fiction and are often dramatized as kinder human beings than their more respectable sisters: "Butterflies, bits of light and song and laughter, dancing, dancing down the last tail-reach of hell."[10]

Those weeks in Dawson netted London many tales and the raw Frontier town appears often in his stories, but it was during the winter in camp that he came to learn about the Alaska of the sourdoughs and of the Indians. It took London and Fred Thompson five days to travel the 80 miles of icy trail back to Split-Up Island in drastically cold weather. (The temperature had dipped to 67 degrees below zero on 29 November.) Having rejoined their companions, they settled down to housekeeping for the winter, or at least part of the winter; London eventually switched cabins after a quarrel over his misuse of one of his companions' ax when chopping ice. London later wrote several colorful articles about living in crowded quarters in a small cabin, in particular "Housekeeping in the Klondike," and many of his stories, in particular "In a Far Country," dramatize vividly the changes it can wreak on those who lack self-control and self-discipline.

Aside from reading Darwin's *On the Origin of Species* and Milton's *Paradise Lost*, both of which he had taken with him up North, and swapping books with his companions, London's favorite recreation was talking and arguing. All his acquaintances on Split-Up Island stressed his enthusiasm for these discussions.[11] Eagerly London questioned the old-timers, listening avidly to their adventures until a picture of Alaska in trail-breaking days grew in his mind. The camp offered a cross-section of the new life that was pulsating through the North: strong men and weaklings, *chekakos* and sourdoughs, homesick family men and adventurers. Of the men who most impressed London, one should mention Louis Savard, a generally silent French Canadian whose accent delighted him, and who had the most comfortable cabin of all. Savard probably was the inspiration for Louis Savoy in *The Son of the Wolf* and for characteristics of both François and Perrault in *The Call of the Wild*, while Nig, Louis's lovable sled-dog who cleverly evaded work, probably became "That Spot" and, according to Joan

London, one of Buck's companions. Emil Jensen, who was 15 years older than London and whom London greatly admired, became the model for the Malemute Kid, London's central and ideal figure in *The Son of the Wolf*, and probably for John Thornton. Finally, there was Stevens, who appears as a teller of tales and all-round adventurer in London's Klondike fiction.

Just how much personal experience London had with Northland dogs is difficult to determine. There were many dogs around, and since the main trail ran near the cabin where he lived, London must have seen some of the best husky teams in the area, probably witnessing more than one prize dog put through the test of breaking a heavily-laden sled out of the ice, whether or not as a result of a bet on the part of his master. He was also familiar with two "outsiders"— Newfoundland and St. Bernard—who learned to hold their own on Split-Up Island: Louis Savard's Nig and Louis Bond's dog Jack, a cross between a St. Bernard and a collie, who became the inspiration for Buck. Marshall and Louis Bond had come to the Klondike from their father Judge Bond's ranch in the Santa Clara Valley, south of San Francisco, bringing two dogs with them, one of whom was Jack. London greatly admired Jack and used his admirable qualities in creating Buck. In Marshall Bond's words, Jack had "characteristics of such excellence as to be not improperly termed character. He had a courage that, though unaggressive, was unyielding; a kindness and good nature that the most urbane man in the world might have observed with profit; and a willingness to do his work, and an untiring energy in carrying it out." It seems that a remarkable relationship established itself between London and Jack:

> London liked these dogs, and in particular this one which I called Jack. His manner of dealing with dogs was different from anyone I ever knew, and I remarked it at the time with interest. Most people, including myself, pat, caress, and talk in more or less affectionate terms to a dog. London did none of this. He always spoke and acted toward the dog as if he recognized his noble qualities, respected them, but took them as a matter of course. As between equals. It always seemed to me that he gave more to the dog than we did, for he gave understanding.[12]

Judge Bond's ranch, which London visited after his return from the Klondike, became Judge Miller's ranch, and Louis Bond himself lent some of his traits to Stanley Prince in *The Son of the Wolf*. In fact, London wrote to Marshall Bond on 17 December 1903: "Yes, Buck is based upon your dog at Dawson. And of course Judge Miller's place was Judge Bond's—even to the cement swimming tank & the artesian well. And don't you remember that your father was attending a meeting of the Fruitgrowers Association the night I visited you, and Louis was organizing an athletic club—all of which events figured with Buck if I remember correctly."[13]

What information London did not have about dogs, he gathered from his readings, and in particular from Egerton R. Young's *My Dogs in the Northland*, published in 1902, only a few months before London started writing *The Call of the Wild*. He probably learned much about the handling and the behavior of sled-dogs from this book, and several of the dogs in *The Call of the Wild* resemble some of Young's dogs, in particular "Young's Jack, a St. Bernard, has some of Buck's feelings of responsibility; Cuffy, a Newfoundland, is not unlike the feminine Curly; the one-eyed husky lead dog Voyageur may have contributed to the portrayal of the unsociable, one-eyed Sol-leks; the behavior of Young's Rover, who constantly licks the wounds of other dogs in the team, may have suggested the role of doctor dog assumed by Skeet" (*Klondike*, 240–41). Although plagiarism would occasionally be charged against London, his use of such sources was merely a use of available data in a technical field and affected neither plot, nor tone, nor theme, nor symbolism. He had visited the territory, he knew what he was describing, he had observed and experienced much, and the data he gathered secondhand were used to fill the gaps of his knowledge and provide realistic detail and a feeling of authenticity.

However, if London's book is well documented, it is not crammed with factual data, for he did not believe in providing too many details that might detract from the "thrust and go" of his story. In fact, he was annoyed at writers who provided too many details. In his otherwise laudatory review of *The Octopus*, London complained of Frank Norris's passion for documentary detail. As far as he was concerned, no one cared "whether Hooven's meat safe be square or oblong; whether it be lined with wire screen or mosquito netting; whether it be hung to the branches of an oak tree or to the ridgepole of the barn; whether, in fact, Hooven has a meat safe or not."[14] London also vigorously defended his own fiction when he was attacked by critics who reproached him with giving insufficient detail, describing his art as "idealized realism"—an art that did not shy away from reality, even in its ugliest aspects, but attempted to grasp the true romance of things at the same time: "When I have drawn a picture in a few strokes, he would spoil it by putting in the multitude of details I have left out. . . . His trouble is that he does not see with a pictorial eye. He merely looks upon a scene and sees every bit of it; but he does not see the true picture in that scene, a picture which can be thrown upon a canvas by eliminating a great mass of things that spoil the composition, that obfuscate the true beautiful lines of it."[15] He saw no contradiction in this; and, for that matter, neither would have Norris, who felt that Zolaesque Naturalism and Romanticism were not far apart.

The influence of heredity and the milieu, the concept of the survival of the fittest and adaptation as the key to survival are overwhelmingly important in *The Call of the Wild*. The book deals less with the concept of evolution than with that of devolution—the return to the primitive of a civilized being when his environment has changed from one of mellow civilization to one of brutality where the only law is: eat or be eaten, kill or be killed.

Until he is kidnapped, Buck has lived the life of a sated aristocrat, king over "all creeping, crawling, flying things of Judge Miller's place, humans included" (44). His education into the harsh realities of an unprotected life begins shortly after he is abducted, and after a two-day-and-night train journey during which he was vilely treated and neither ate nor drank. After having changed hands several times and in a fever of pain and rage, Buck meets the man in the red sweater who is the first step of his initiation into the wild: the dog breaker. Buck had never been struck with a club in his life, but again and again with each new charge he is brought crushingly to the ground by a vicious blow of the club. Although his rage knows no bounds and although he is a large, powerful dog, he is no match against a man who is "no slouch at dog-breakin'" and knows how to handle a club efficiently. The man in the red sweater finishes Buck with a blow directly on the nose and a final "shrewd blow" that knocks him unconscious. Buck thus learns his first lesson: that a man with a club is a master to be obeyed, although not necessarily conciliated. "That club was a revelation. It was his introduction to the reign of primitive law, and he met the introduction half-way" (51). Buck, however, retains his dignity and never fawns on his masters. They are stronger than he is; therefore, in order to survive, he obeys them. Having seen a dog who would neither obey nor conciliate killed in the struggle for mastery made the alternatives clear to him: to obey, to conciliate, or to die. The lesson is enforced each time Buck watches another dog being broken. A survivor above all else, Buck knows he is beaten, but his spirit is never broken.

Buck's next lesson takes place on Dyea Beach when Curly, whom he has befriended, is killed by the huskies when she makes advances to one of them in her usual friendly way. In two minutes, she is literally torn to pieces. "So that was the way. No fair play. Once down, that was the end of you. Well [Buck] would see to it that he never went down" (56). This traumatic lesson often returns to haunt Buck's sleep. There seems to be only one law in this new world that both men and beasts obey—the law of club and fang—and like Dave and Sol-leks, one has to learn to give nothing, ask for nothing, and expect nothing.

Adapting to a new environment also entails learning other lessons, not only simple lessons such as digging a hole in the snow to sleep in or eating quickly to leave no one the time to steal his food, but also lessons involving moral changes. Buck learns to steal, and London makes it clear that his first theft marked Buck as fit to survive in the hostile Northland environment. "It marked his adaptability, his capacity to adjust himself to changing conditions, the lack of which would have meant swift and terrible death. It marked, further, the decay or going to pieces of his moral nature, a vain thing and a handicap in the ruthless struggle for existence" (62–63). London comments with some irony that, while living on Judge Miller's estate, Buck would have died for a moral principle, such as the defense of the Judge's riding whip, but that "the completeness of his decivilization was now evidenced by his ability to flee from the defense of a moral consideration and so save his hide" (63). Among other moral qualities Buck sheds are his sense of fair play and of mercy, which are things reserved for gentler climates. In the wilderness of the North, survival is the only goal and ruthlessness the only way to survive. Thus, Buck learns through experience and proves that he is eminently adaptable and fit. His body also adapts well to the new demands of the environment: he loses his fastidiousness, grows callous to pain, achieves an internal as well as an external economy, making the most of whatever comes his way, his senses develop to an incredible acuteness, and forgotten instincts come to life in him. Indeed, heredity also plays an important role in his survival:

> And not only did he learn by experience, but instincts long dead became alive again. The domesticated generations fell from him. In vague ways he remembered back to the youth of the breed, to the time the wild dogs ranged in packs through the primeval forest and killed their meat as they ran it down. It was no task for him to learn to fight with cut and slash and the quick wolf snap. In this manner had fought forgotten ancestors. They quickened the old life within him, and the old tricks which they had stamped into the heredity of the breed were his tricks. They came to him without effort or discovery, as though they had been his always. (64)

This link with a remote past when men and dogs were wild is the major theme running throughout the book and is handled by London not only as a naturalistic theme but also as a mythical and archetypal one.

Since the wolf is a predator, the basic instinct coming to life in Buck is the instinct to kill—an instinct of which he was not originally conscious. He progresses fast, beginning with small game and, eventually, killing man. The instinct to kill, as London makes clear, is common to all predators, and man himself has not completely lost it and indulges it when he goes shooting or hunting. However, for Buck, the killing is infinitely more intimate because it is not carried out by proxy through a bullet: "He was ranging at the head of the pack, running the wild thing down, the living meat, to kill with his own teeth and wash his muzzle to the eyes in warm blood" (76). Although it is Spitz, instead of Buck, who kills the snowshoe rabbit, its death marks the awakening of Buck's own desire to kill, and he immediately challenges

Spitz to a fight to the death—a fight Buck wins largely because the knowledge of ancestral fighting techniques becomes his instantly: "As they circled about, snarling, ears laid back, keenly watchful for the advantage, the scene came to Buck with a sense of familiarity. He seemed to remember it all—the white woods, and earth, and moonlight, and the thrill of battle. . . . To Buck it was nothing new or strange, this scene of old time. It was as though it had always been, the wonted way of things" (78). After defeating Spitz, and while the pack has closed in upon his crippled enemy, "Buck stood and looked on, the successful champion, the dominant primordial beast who had made his kill and found it good" (80). Buck has indeed now come of age, and although his education is not finished, he has proven that he is one of the fit.

Once Buck has proven himself on the hereditary and environmental levels and has reverted to instinctual patterns of behavior, his life with a new master, John Thornton, suddenly becomes more mellow and affords him the opportunity to relax his vigilance. But Buck cannot return to his old self, for he has learned only too well the lessons of the wild—that one should never forgo an advantage or draw back from a fight one has started, that mercy is misunderstood for fear or weakness, and that such misunderstanding makes for death. He has gained knowledge from the depth of Time, and such knowledge cannot be discarded once it has become part of the conscious self. Thus, his life with John Thornton, which could, in other circumstances, have heralded a return to the tame, is merely an interval in Buck's evolution, and the call of the wild keeps summoning him until he has returned fully to the life of his ancestors, until he has become part of nature.

In the last stages of Buck's evolution or devolution, London's handling of the theme of heredity becomes more and more mythical and archetypal. As the "blood longing" becomes stronger in him, Buck fights larger and larger prey and begins to look more and more like his wild brothers, transforming himself in the secrecy of the forest into a thing of the wild, "stealing along softly, cat-footed, a passing shadow that appeared and disappeared among the shadows" (131). Buck kills a large black bear and a huge bull moose he stalks and worries for four days before finally pulling him down with the dogged, tireless, persistent patience of the wild when it hunts its living food. Then, out of despair and anger at the murder of John Thornton, Buck attacks and kills men—the Yeehats who have massacred Thornton's party—kills them in the face of the law of club and fang. His last ties with mankind being broken, Buck is now free to join and lead a pack of wolves and live the life of the wild to the fullest.

From the standpoints of documentation and major themes, *The Call of the Wild* is indeed a naturalistic novel. According to the criteria of noninvolvement and objectivity, the story is still rather naturalistic; but in the areas of amorality and rejection of social taboos it is naturalistic by default, for Buck's gorgeous coat of fur allows London to deal uninhibitedly with themes he would otherwise shun. Indeed, many painful and shocking scenes are described by London with perfect objectivity. Among such scenes is the potentially heartrending scene in which Buck is beaten by the man in the red sweater, which is rendered in detail but with no expression of sympathy or pity on London's part. Nor does London dwell on Buck's pain. He merely describes accurately what the man does to Buck and how Buck reacts. The fight between Buck and Spitz, the death of Dave, the stalking and the killing of the bull moose, Buck's standing off the wolf pack, are all scenes London handles with perfect objectivity, never indulging in expressions of emotion or pity. He even indicates with remarkable simplicity the economy-of-pain principle upon which the moose herd functions, and how they are ready to pay the price of one head so that the herd might be freed from Buck's menacing presence: "Besides, it was not the life of the herd, or of the young bulls, that was threatened. The life of only one member was demanded, which was a remoter interest in their lives, and in the end they were content to pay the toll" (133).

Pain, suffering, and death, London can describe unemotionally. Love, however, is another matter, but Buck's furry nature allows London not to wax romantic. Although he describes Buck's passionate devotion to John Thornton in abstract terms, he never allows Buck to lose his dignity and fawn upon his master as the other dogs do. The various instances when Buck proves his love for his master, whether it be by attempting to jump over a chasm (which would have been certain death), by attacking "Black" Burton, by risking his own life repeatedly in the rapids to save Thornton's, or, finally, by pulling a sleigh loaded with 1,000 pounds of flour, are always described with a great economy of emotion. London merely describes Buck's actions; love in action, not as an emotion. What expression of feeling London dramatizes is on the part of Thornton. Indeed, the men are awed by the length to which Buck will carry his devotion to Thornton, and Thornton is the one who expresses his love for Buck after the latter has won his bet for him. "Thornton fell on his knees beside Buck. Head was against head, and he was shaking him back and forth. Those who hurried up heard him cursing Buck, and he cursed him long and fervently, and softly and lovingly" (121). The amoral stance of the novel is an easy one for London to carry out since the perfect logic of Buck's reversal to the wild is easily acceptable on the part of an animal. It would be far more difficult to accept on the part of a human being, especially by London's early-twentieth-century audience. The needs of the poor-young-American-girls-who-must-not-be-shocked tend to limit the naturalistic point of view of many of his stories dealing with human protagonists, and many of the themes London dramatizes easily in *The Call of the Wild* are present but transformed in his other fiction. While we are ready to accept Buck's loss of moral principles as a necessary part of his survival, it would be more difficult to do so if Buck were a human protagonist, and London never condones it for his two-legged characters. In fact, in his stories of the North, survival for man calls for virtues such as courage, integrity, and brotherhood. Like dogs, men must change both physically and morally since only the strong shall survive; but they must change for the better morally as well as physically, and, as London makes clear in stories such as "In a Far Country," they must substitute for the courtesies of ordinary life "unselfishness, forbearance, and tolerance." Those who fail usually die a useless and shameful death, after having lived without dignity, such as the protagonists of "In a Far Country" and the miserably incompetent Hal, Charles, and Mercedes in *The Call of the Wild*, who neither "toil hard, suffer sore, and remain sweet of speech and kindly" (99). Indeed, they embody the very antithesis of what man should be in the wilderness of the North if he is to survive. London's ideal hero of *The*

Son of the Wolf and *The God of His Fathers*, Malemute Kid, resembles John Thornton in most ways. Unlike Buck, these men have not lost their moral nature.

Despite this basic difference in London's dramatization of men and beasts, there are numerous points in common, and many scenes in *The Call of the Wild* have their parallel in London's other fiction of the North. Buck's blood lust and the enjoyment he experiences in fighting a worthy opponent is paralleled, for instance, by Scruff Mackenzie's fight in "The Son of the Wolf": "At first he felt compassion for his enemy; but this fled before the primal instinct of life, which in turn gave way to the lust of slaughter. The ten thousand years of culture fell from him, and he was a cave-dweller, doing battle for his female."[16] Buck's stalking of the bull moose, and the way he prevents the poor animal from getting food, drink or rest, reminds one of Thomas Stephens's victimization of the mammoth in "A Relic of the Pliocene," but also of the more gripping "Law of Life." Finally, for both men and dogs, only one quality can make for survival when all else is equal: imagination. It is imagination that allows Buck to win his fight with Spitz, when both dogs are equally matched; and the lack of imagination that causes the death of the man in "To Build a Fire." Patience and imagination have nothing to do with great physical strength or moral nature; but for both men and dogs their absence can make for death.

Indeed, in London's wilderness in the North, a man's world and a dog's world have much in common, and both are ruled by naturalistic laws; but in the "dog stories" such as *The Call of the Wild* or "Bâtard" London can go further, for he is not hindered by the moral requirements of his audience. He can never quite handle human protagonists with the same amoral, objective stance.

7

Buck and Carl Jung's Archetypes of the Collective Unconscious

When reviewers interpreted *The Call of the Wild* as a brilliant human allegory, London commented that he was unconscious of having written a human allegory at the time and that it was "a purely fortuitous piece of work, a lucky shot in the dark that had unexpectedly found its mark" (*Times*, 252), unknowingly using a most appropriate metaphor. *The Call of the Wild* is indeed a shot in the "dark," that is, in the darkness of the unconscious, in a world of myth and Jungian archetypes. Small wonder that London discovered Jung's work at the end of his life and 13 years after having written *The Call of the Wild* with a flash of recognition and that he felt Jung had expressed in psychological terms what he had himself striven to dramatize throughout his work. Intellectually and rationally satisfying because of its successful Naturalism, the novel is also psychologically and emotionally gratifying because it offers the reader's unconscious a vision of a perfectly integrated personality as well as a set of harmonious primordial images and archetypes, thus allowing complete identification with Buck on the level of the unconscious. Actually, it seems that London unwittingly dug deep into his own personal and collective unconscious to capture a forgotten but vital aspect of the human psyche that he communicates to his readers through his portrayal of Buck on both conscious and unconscious levels—the unconscious communication giving depth and power to the conscious one, just as the stateliness and enormous power of an iceberg resides not in the one-eighth that is above water but in the seven-eighths below water.

Almost every step of Jung's study of the human psyche seems to apply to Buck, and most conflicts are resolved in him. In fact, Buck provides the libido with perfect fulfillment, offering a perfect harmonization of the progression and regression principles; he provides the shadow with free range and is able to listen to both his personal and his collective unconscious; both his shadow and his persona eventually merge harmoniously; and he satisfies most major archetypal urges and is one with archetypal images. A tall order to fill, but one which Buck fills with all the grace and comfort of his gorgeous fur coat. Buck's furry nature is constantly emphasized by London and is vital to our identification with and acceptance of him. Indeed, on the conscious level, we would find it more difficult to identify with him completely if he were a two-legged, smooth-skinned creature.

Carl Jung's conception of the *psyche*, a term which he uses to cover both the conscious and the unconscious, is that of a system which is at the same time dynamic, in constant movement, and self-regulating. He calls the psychic energy *libido*, in the general sense of "longing" or "urge." The libido flows between opposing poles, and Jung calls the forward movement, which is intended to satisfy the demands of the conscious, *progression*, and the backward movement, which is intended to satisfy the demands of the unconscious, *regression*. Progression involves the active adaptation to one's environment; regression the adaptation to one's inner needs. Both are perfectly normal, although they are often perceived as conflicting. A man must be in harmony both with his environment and with himself, one conditioning the other. A man can only "adapt to his inner world and achieve harmony with himself when he is adapted to the environmental conditions,"[1] and vice versa. Unfortunately, man living in society finds conciliating both needs difficult because the demands of society often thwart the demands of the self. For Buck, however, it is quite differ-

ent. In fact, the more he adapts to the demands of the harsh environment of the North, the better he adapts to his own inner world; con-
versely, the more he listens to his inner yearnings, the fitter he is to
deal with his environment because the inner voice he listens to is that
of a being in perfect harmony with his environment.

The key to this harmony is, of course, the fact that the new
world Buck needs to adapt to is a primitive, primordial world, and
that, in order to adapt to it, he needs to listen to the instincts he has
inherited from his forefathers. London understood clearly that Buck's
progress in adapting to his environment was in fact a regression into
his instinctive past, what Jung would call his *collective unconscious*:
"His development (or retrogression) was rapid. . . . And when, on the
still, cold nights, he pointed his nose at a star and howled long and
wolflike, it was his ancestors, dead and dust, pointing nose at star and
howling down through the centuries and through him. And his
cadences were their cadences, the cadences which voiced their woes
and what to them was the meaning of the stillness, and the cold, and
the dark" (63). For Buck, the hard-won values of the conscious and
the vitality and power of the unconscious are no longer at war, and
adaptation to his environment involves adopting a new set of values
which enhances rather than thwarts the vitality of his unconscious,
thus satisfying fully his libido.

For Jung, the *ego* is the center of consciousness, the knowing,
willing "I," the conscious factor by excellence. It is never more and
never less than consciousness as a whole. The *self*, on the other hand,
is the center of the totality of the personality, including both conscious
and unconscious—personal unconscious as well as collective unconscious. The ego is part of the whole, and the self is the whole. The
unconscious is divided into three levels: "first, temporary subliminal
contents that can be reproduced voluntarily (memory); second, unconscious contents that cannot be reproduced voluntarily; third, contents
that are not capable of becoming conscious at all"[2]—except, occasionally, through dreams. The personal unconscious is the second level of
the unconscious. It is the sum of one's repressed infantile impulses and
wishes, subliminal perceptions (perceptions of insufficient strength to
reach consciousness, experiences which are only partly comprehended

and of which one is not fully aware), and countless forgotten experiences. It belongs to the individual alone and is acquired through his lifetime. The collective unconscious—the third level of the unconscious—is a deeper stratum of the unconscious. It is inherited and manifests itself through instinctive behavior (instincts being defined as "impulses to action without conscious motivation") (*Jung*, 23). Every human being possesses a personal unconscious and, at the same time, participates in the collective unconscious. The human brain has been shaped by the remote experiences of mankind and apprehends reality in a manner conditioned by the past history of mankind. Jung tried to clarify the concept by comparing the psyche to the human body: "just as the human body shows a common anatomy over and above all racial differences so, too, the psyche possesses a common substratum transcending all differences in culture and consciousness. I have called this substratum the collective unconscious. This unconscious psyche, common to all mankind, does not consist merely of contents capable of becoming conscious, but of latent dispositions toward identical reactions."[3] This is what Jung calls archetypal perception; the archetypes being an inborn form of intuition or perception, of which we are unconscious but which forces our apprehension and experience of life into specific human patterns. Archetypes are experienced as emotions as well as images and were probably formed during the thousands of years when the human brain and consciousness were emerging from the animal. Archetypes are essentially the contents of the collective unconscious.

Jung defines seven major archetypes: the persona, the shadow, the anima and the animus, the old wise man, the earth mother, and the self, most of which seem to apply to *The Call of the Wild* and to Buck's experience. However, Buck satisfies not only his own persona, shadow, and self but also permits the reader to identify with a completely integrated personality and with a godlike archetype of the self that transcends all religious barriers because of its inherent amorality.

The process of civilizing the individual involves the formation of a mask behind which the real person lives. This mask is the persona and comprises all the characteristics and qualities expected of the individual in his chosen position.

Society expects, and indeed must expect, every individual to play the part assigned to him as perfectly as possible, so that a man who is a parson . . . must at all times . . . play the role of parson in a flawless manner. Each must stand at his post, here a cobbler, there a poet. No man is expected to be both . . . that would be "odd." Such a man would be "different" from other people, not quite reliable. . . . [I]n short he would always be suspected of unreliability and incompetence, because society is persuaded that only the cobbler who is not a poet can supply workmanlike shoes.[4]

People who do not conform to the norm are often discriminated against and persecuted. The persona is therefore collective and protective. While it is often mistaken for individuality, it is in fact the opposite of individuality because it is a socially manufactured mask that might equally well belong to somebody else. The persona also inhibits and controls the rest of the personality, in particular the shadow.

The shadow is the other side of the personality repressed by the persona. It is the primitive, uncontrolled, vital, and animal part of ourselves. It is both our personal unconscious—"the uncivilized desires and emotions that are incompatible with social standards or our ideal personality, all that we are ashamed of, all that we do not want to know about ourselves" (*Jung*, 50)—and a collective phenomenon that includes part of our collective unconscious. We must accept the existence of our shadow and learn to live with it. Mental and physical health depends on it, and the backlash of repressing it too rigidly can be very destructive and may manifest itself in uncontrolled outbursts of violence or, at the extreme, in insanity. The heavy price to be paid for a nearly complete repression of the shadow is dramatized vividly by Doris Lessing in "To Room Nineteen," where a young woman who has lived a model social life loses her mind and commits suicide without ever really knowing why. Because she has identified completely with her persona and entirely denied her deeper needs, the literal revenge of her repressed shadow is to make her withdraw from life entirely.

At the beginning of the *The Call of the Wild*, Buck's persona is his civilized, nice-dog personality. On Judge Miller's place, in the

Santa Clara Valley, his life is one of peace and quiet happiness, where his shadow is basically denied. His relationship with humans is civilized: "With the Judge's sons, hunting and tramping, it [is] a working partnership; with the Judge's grandsons, a sort of pompous guardianship; and with the Judge himself, a stately and dignified friendship" (108). In fact, Buck's life on the ranch—that of a sated aristocrat, "king over all creeping, crawling, flying things of Judge Miller's place, humans included" (44)—is a paradise for the conscious mind. He enjoys a great deal of freedom and comfort, many privileges, and some responsibilities, and he is totally unaware that he is only half alive, for no passion of any kind enters his world.

Later, in the North, after he has been tested and has proved himself a survivor, after his shadow has been awakened and is no longer completely repressed by his conscious mind, Buck's persona changes, and his personality is more integrated in that his shadow becomes a vital part of his psyche. He now functions actively on both conscious and unconscious levels. His new social persona of sled-dog dedicated to hard work and survival allows for the expression of the shadow; not only allows it but demands it, since it is a world in which survival involves working to the limits of one's strength, enduring pain, facing death, and confronting others in a continuous struggle where losing means immediate death at the teeth of the pack. This is not a world the civilized persona is able to deal with, as the swift death of Curly makes clear. It is a world for the shadow; and only those who allow their shadow to surface and take over in times of stress do survive. Buck's new ego now gives equal power to his persona and his shadow, and his new self is equally balanced between conscious and unconscious drives, the vitality and power of his unconscious predominating more and more as time passes.

It is the emergence of his collective unconscious added to his physical power and intelligence that allows Buck to survive. This collective unconscious warns him of danger and gives him the tools and techniques necessary to defeat his adversaries. His instant recognition of what might be a trap is a clear instance of behavior controlled by instinctive knowledge arising from the collective unconscious: "The snow pressed him on every side, and a great surge of fear swept through him—the fear of the wild thing for the trap. It was a token that he was harking back through his own life to the lives of his fore-bears; for he was a civilized dog, an unduly civilized dog, and of his own experience knew no trap and so could not of himself fear it" (59). Buck's newly discovered ability to bide his time "with a patience that [is] nothing short of primitive" (72) is also evidence of his collective unconscious and is characteristic of predators whose only hope to eat and survive resides in their ability to lie in wait until their potential victim or foe is vulnerable. The way Buck saps Spitz's authority with the pack and eventually defeats him evidences a perfect balance of social wherewithal and of behavior controlled by the unconscious. He fulfills his role as a sled-dog to perfection, while demoralizing and humiliating Spitz socially in a way that is undetectable by their masters. It is only François's instinctive understanding that tells him what Buck is up to: "François knew he was behind the trouble, and Buck knew that he knew; but Buck was too clever ever again to be caught red-handed. He worked faithfully in the harness, for the toil had become a delight to him; yet it was a greater delight slyly to precipitate a fight amongst his mates and tangle the traces" (76). Then, when the time is ripe, he strikes and wins.

Throughout most of the story, Buck's persona and shadow are in equilibrium. He fulfills a social role where work is all important and, at the same time, he is in tune with his instincts. His new hard-won values are not in opposition with his vitality and power. Much to the contrary, he is now more fully alive than he ever was on Judge Miller's ranch:

> There is an ecstasy that marks the summit of life, and beyond which life cannot rise. And such is the paradox of living, this ecstasy comes when one is most alive, and it comes as a complete forgetfulness that one is alive. . . . [A]nd it came to Buck, leading the pack, sounding the wolf cry, straining after the food that was alive and that fled before him through the moon-light. He was sounding the deeps of his nature, and of the parts of his nature that were deeper than he, going back into the womb of Time. He was mastered by the sheer surging of life, the tidal wave of being, the perfect joy of each separate muscle, joint, and sinew in that it

was everything that was not death, that it was aglow and rampant, expressing itself in movement, flying exultantly under the stars and over the face of dead matter that did not move. (76–77)

Buck lived a life of quiet happiness in California; in the Northland, he now lives intensely every aspect of life, be it pain, joy, love, hatred, or work. Buck has discovered passion, which is a manifestation of the shadow: an intense hatred of Spitz and an ardent love of John Thornton—"Love, genuine passionate love, was his for the first time. . . . [L]ove that was feverish and burning, that was adoration, that was madness, it had taken John Thornton to arouse" (108).

Work is the organizing principle of this new social order, and, like the other dogs, Buck has been gripped by the pride of the trail and trace, "that pride which holds dogs in the toil to the last gasp, which lures them to die joyfully in the harness and breaks their heart if they are cut out of the harness. This was the pride of Dave as wheel dog, of Sol-leks as he pulled with all his strength; the pride that laid hold of them at break of camp, transforming them from sour and sullen brutes into straining, eager, ambitious creatures" (72). It is that persona assumed with a passion that makes poor Dave insist on working despite the pain of internal injury and still attempt to crawl to his feet to be harnessed when all strength has left him. In fact, despite its monotony, work for these dogs has become "the supreme expression of their being, and all that they lived for and the only thing in which they took delight" (60).

The third stage of Buck's evolution involves the shedding of this new social persona and the adoption of a third and final persona: a mythical or archetypal persona that becomes the very embodiment of his shadow. But, for a while, living with John Thornton, Buck seems to take on a double personality represented by his dog/wolf duality. Clearly his dog personality is the embodiment of his persona, while his wolf personality is that of his shadow: "But in spite of this great love he bore John Thornton, which seemed to bespeak the soft, civilizing influence, the strain of the primitive, which the Northland had aroused in him, remained alive and active. Faithfulness and devotion, things born of fire and roof, were his; yet he retained his wildness and wiliness. He was a thing of the wild, come in from the wild, to sit by John Thornton's fire, rather than a dog of the soft Southland stamped with the marks of generations of civilization" (110). Even his physical behavior, and in particular his way of walking, changes as he changes personalities. While in camp and living with humans, he marches; but, as soon as he leaves camp, "he [becomes] a thing of the wild, stealing along softly, cat-footed, a passing shadow that appear[s] and disappear[s] among the shadows" (131).

There are two calls luring him: the physical call, the conscious call of the wild, which is the call of other wolves in the forest; and the psychological call of the primitive, the largely unconscious call of the archetypes, which manifests itself much earlier. In fact, toward the end of the book, when Buck is ready to hear it and understand it, the psychological call of the wild materializes itself into the physical call of the wolf: "a long-drawn howl, like, yet unlike, any noise made by a husky dog. And he knew it, in the old familiar way, as a sound heard before" (126). The cry of the wolf is part of Buck's collective memory, buried in his collective unconscious. When he responds to it and meets up with a real wolf, he feels in tune with that puzzling yearning that has been luring him for so long: "He knew he was at last answering the call, running by the side of his wood brother toward the place from where the call surely came. Old memories were coming upon him fast, and he was stirring to them as of old he stirred to the realities of which they were the shadows. He had done this thing before, somewhere in that other and dimly remembered world, and he was doing it again, now, running free in the open, the unpacked earth underfoot, the wide sky overhead" (128). What Buck clearly does not know is that the call he has been hearing did not come from anywhere outside of him, but from his collective unconscious, and that answering the call of the wolf was doing what he had deeply yearned to do without being aware of it. It was not him but his ancestors in a remote past who had run free the way he is now running. Buck has now not only fulfilled the needs of his shadow but also answered the call of his collective unconscious.

When Buck is ready to discard his social persona, the man who linked him to the civilized world is killed and disappears from his life if not from his memory. Buck's social self thus becomes a useless thing that can be discarded without regret. His shadow and unconscious now have free range. Interestingly, his earlier personas of companion dog and of sled-dog now recede further and further into his personal unconscious. With the passing of years, he only pays tribute to the latter religiously once a year, on the anniversary of John Thornton's death: "In the summers there is one visitor, however, to that valley. . . . It is a great, gloriously coated wolf, like, and yet unlike, all others. He crosses alone from the smiling timber land and comes down into an open space among the trees. Here a yellow stream flows from rotted moose-hide sacks and sinks into the ground, with the long grasses growing through it and vegetable mold overrunning it and hiding its yellow from the sun; and here he muses for a time, howling once, long and mournfully, ere he departs" (139–40). His new persona is now that of a wolf, and his personal unconscious includes his civilized self.

Dreams are messages from the unconscious, and their function is "to try to restore our psychological balance by producing dream material that re-establishes, in a subtle way, the total psychic equilibrium."[5] Dreams often compensate for the deficiencies of our personalities, may warn us of the danger of our present course, and may sometimes announce certain situations long before they take place. It seems that Buck's dreams prepare him for what is to come and draw his attention to his inner call. While snoozing by the fireside, he sometimes remembers Judge Miller's place in California; but more often his half-dreams have their roots in his collective unconscious and hark back to the dawn of humanity:

> Sometimes as he crouched there, blinking dreamily at the flames, it seemed that the flames were of another fire, and that as he crouched by this other fire he saw another and different man from the half-breed cook before him. This other man was shorter of leg and long of arm, with muscles that were stringy and knotted rather than rounded and swelling. The hair of this man was long and matted, and his head slanted back under it from the eyes. He uttered strange sounds and seemed very much afraid of the darkness, into which he peered continually, clutching in his hand,

which hung midway between knee and foot, a stick with a heavy stone made fast to the end. . . . At other times this hairy man squatted by the fire with head between his legs and slept. . . . And beyond the fire, in the circling darkness, Buck could see many gleaming coals, two by two, always two by two, which he knew to be the eyes of great beasts of prey. (86–87)

This symbolic dream, which harks back to the Stone Age, is what Freud would call an "archaic remnant" and what Jung calls a primordial image or an archetype. It reminds Buck of his ancestral past, of the first dogs that sat by a man's fireside, of a past when both primitive man and dog could only survive through strength and cunning, and when both were governed by instincts. It is also telling Buck that this is the way he must now live and suggests that he too may become one of the great beasts of prey. As Buck is drawn more and more powerfully to the wild, the call of the primitive becomes louder and more insistent and the dream of the short hairy man recurs more often, "filling him with a great unrest and strange desires" (125).

Indeed the harsh and primitive environment of the Far North brings out Buck's primordial urges and archetypal images. As he is able to satisfy these urges and become one with these images, he achieves a perfect integration of the self, eventually becoming himself the ultimate archetype of the self: a God-image. Primordial urges are both simple and vital: they are the urge to survive, to eat, to kill, and to mate. These urges, which in social life are usually satisfied indirectly through work, sports (violent sports and hunting, in particular), and marriage, find a more basic fulfillment in the wild, and Buck finds more pleasure in satisfying them in a primitive fashion than he ever did in a "civilized" one. Survival and killing, which had not been issues on Judge Miller's ranch, are the foremost issues in the North, and learning to satisfy them brings out Buck's racial memory:

With the aurora borealis flaming coldly overhead . . . this song of the huskies might have been the defiance of life, only it was pitched in minor key, with long-drawn wailings and half-sobs, and was more the pleading of life, the articulate travail of existence. It was an old song, old as the breed itself—one of the first songs of the younger world in a day when songs were sad. It was invested with the woe of unnumbered generations, this plaint by which Buck was so strangely stirred. When he moaned and sobbed, it was with the pain of living that was of old the pain of his wild fathers, and the fear and mystery of the cold and dark that was to them fear and mystery. And that he should be stirred by it marked the completeness with which he harked back through the ages of fire and roof to the raw beginnings of life in the howling ages. (74)

The greatest and most powerful experience for Buck is that of killing, of running down his food, and eating what he has killed—a far cry from a dish of dog-food at Judge Miller's ranch. In such moments, Buck is perfectly at one with his self and with nature, experiencing a feeling of wholeness and completion which no civilized experience ever matched in intensity: "The blood longing became stronger than ever before. He was a killer, a thing that preyed, living on the things that lived, unaided, alone, by virtue of his own strength and prowess, surviving triumphantly in a hostile environment where only the strong survived. . . . Life streamed through him in splendid flood, glad and rampant, until it seemed that it would burst him asunder in sheer ecstasy and pour forth generously over the world" (129–30). He is doing what his forefathers did for millions of years, and he has become an integral part of nature. "He linked the past with the present, and the eternity behind him throbbed through him in a mighty rhythm to which he swayed as the tides and seasons swayed" (110–11). He stands for the fulfillment of the self, having brought the process of individuation—the conscious coming to terms with one's inner center—into reality. In fact, starting with Buck's painful realization at the hands of the man with the red sweater that he was not as powerful as he thought, the whole story describes his progress toward individuation. Mating, which had never been on his mind, eventually comes to him naturally when he has become the leader of a pack of wolves. Since the satisfaction of this particular instinct is in no way the focus of the story, London merely suggests it when he tells us that the Yeehats "noted a change in the breed of timber wolves; for some were seen with splashes of brown on head and muzzle, and with a rift of white centering down the chest (139)"—clearly indicating Buck's paternity. For humans, however, individuation is never complete. In the civilized world, one cannot shed successfully all the masks, and "the manifestation in life of one's innate, inborn potentialities" cannot be realized fully or on a permanent basis, the "individuating ego com[ing] again and again to points where it must transcend its previous image of itself."[6]

Buck himself becomes at the end of the novel the most powerful archetype of the wholeness of the self, and, wisely, the tale ends there, with a remarkable visual image: "When the long winter nights come on and wolves follow their meat into the lower valleys, he may be seen running at the head of the pack through the pale moonlight or glimmering borealis, leaping gigantic above his fellows, his great throat a-bellow as he sings a song of the younger world, which is the song of the pack" (129–30). Buck becomes a pagan and vengeful God who terrorizes the Yeehats, for whom he is now a Ghost Dog and an Evil Spirit who has no fear of men and who, they believe, has selected the valley where they murdered John Thornton as his abiding place.

Carl Jung explains that the concept of the self and that of a God-image are virtually indistinguishable. In fact, if the shadow belongs to "the realm of bodiless phantoms," the self is completely outside of the personal sphere and appears only through its symbols. Symbols of unity and totality are usually symbols of the self. However, completeness and perfection are not the same thing. For instance, Christ is perfection but is only a symbol of one half of the self (the positive half), the self without its shadow. He is a glorified man, a son of God, "unspotted by sin," Adam before the Fall. The other half, the shadow, is symbolized by the Antichrist. Therefore, Christ plus Antichrist, both Christian symbols, form a complete symbol of the self. Other symbols of the wholeness of the self are *mandalas*, which mean circles, and more especially magic circles. *The Call of the Wild* features a number of mandalas. In fact, every time Buck is tested, the test takes place inside a mandala, which is most appropriate since mandalas are symbols of order and occur in individuals during times of psychic disorientation or reorientation (*Aion*, 28–29). Animals are also seen as archetypes of the self, representing our instinctive nature and its connectedness with our surroundings. Not surprisingly, they were often worshipped as Gods in antiquity. In fact, animals and groups of four (mandalas) are universal religious symbols. Many primitive civilizations believed that man "has a 'bush soul' as well as his own, and that this bush soul is incarnate in a wild animal or a tree with which the human individual has some kind of psychic identity" ("Approaching," 6–7), and primitive people will often describe mental derangements as "the loss of a soul," meaning a disruption of consciousness. In a sense, modern man has lost his (bush) soul, in that he has lost his sense of connectedness with nature, what Lucien Lévy-Bruhl called "mystic participation," which explains why animals as symbols of the self still haunt our dreams, showing that our unconscious is trying to reestablish that lost link. "The 'inwardness' of each animal reaches far out into the world around it and 'psychifies' time and space. In ways that are still completely beyond our comprehension, our unconscious is similarly attuned to our surroundings—to our group, to society in general, and, beyond these, to the space-time continuum and the whole of nature."[7] Clearly, Buck as godlike and wild-animal symbol of the self comes to symbolize for the reader and for his creator not only the integration of the personality but also the reintegration of the modern self into nature.

Neither does Buck understand what is happening to him nor did London know the kind of symbol he was creating in Buck, or that he was in fact describing a vital psychological process through the story of the dog. Buck is merely living the experience, and not reasoning it out. What London tells us about him is perfectly coherent with dog behavior, and he seldom projects upon him a human intelligence. In fact, he is at some pains to point out on several occasions that Buck is unaware of what is happening to him—or rather that he feels without understanding them the hidden reasons behind his yearnings. For instance, when the mysterious call drawing him into the forest is becoming more insistent and compels him to turn his back "upon the fire and the beaten earth around it, and to plunge into the forest, and on and on, he knew not where or why; nor did he wonder where or why" (111).

Buck is actually rather confused about the whole experience, and he mistakes his inner call for an outer call:

> Sometimes he pursued the call into the forest, looking for it as though it were a tangible thing, barking softly or defiantly, as the mood might dictate. He would thrust his nose into the cool wood moss, or into the black soil where the long grasses grew, and snort with joy at the fat earth smells; or he would crouch for hours, as if in concealment. . . . It might be, lying thus, that he hoped to surprise this call he could not understand. But he did not know why he did these various things. He was impelled to do them, and did not reason about them at all. (125–26)

It is not Buck's conscious mind which guides his behavior, but his unconscious. He behaves exactly as humans when they do something for no apparent reason, and then wonder what got into them. Except that Buck does not wonder what got into him. London felt that although one knows nothing about what dogs think, one may "conclude from their actions what their mental processes might be" and that "such conclusions may be within the range of possibility."[8]

London himself could only have been guided largely by his own unconscious when he wrote the story, for one does not invent consciously such a natural symbol as Buck or describe so vividly the integration of the shadow and the realization of the personal and the collective unconscious with full awareness. "Under certain conditions the unconscious spontaneously brings forth an archetypal symbol of wholeness"(*Aion*, 59), which is clearly what happened to London in 1903. He knew he wanted to write a dog story to redeem the species after the publication in 1902 of "Diable—A Dog," which dramatized the revenge of a dog mistreated by a vicious master. He also knew, as he was writing *The Call of the Wild*, that the story was unlike any other dog story and that he could not stop writing it—that the story had, in fact, taken over and was writing itself (one might add, very much as the spontaneous manifestation of a dream). But the symbolical and mythical power of Buck could only have been a message from London's unconscious.

One may find it difficult to accept that a writer should not be fully aware of the implications of his writing and feel threatened by the idea that the conscious mind is not fully in control of one's life and actions. But great works of art always include an expression of the author's unconscious. Jack London and Edgar Allan Poe are American writers whose work is deeply archetypal, and whose symbolical expression has struck a responding chord in the whole world, if not always with the American critical establishment. In fact, to use Jung's own words, "No genius has ever sat down with a pen or a brush in his hand and said: 'Now I am going to invent a symbol.' No one can take a more or less rational thought . . . and then give it 'symbolic' form. No matter what fantastic trappings one may put upon an idea of this kind, it will remain a sign, linked to the conscious thought behind it, not a symbol that hints at something not yet known,"–the difference between a sign and a symbol being that a sign is always less than the concept it represents, while a symbol stands for something more than its obvious and immediate meaning ("Approaching," 41). Symbols emanate from the unconscious, and an ability to recognize them mirrors a willingness to accept the unconscious.

"Natural" symbols are derived from the unconscious contents of the psyche and can be "traced back to their archaic roots—that is, to ideas and images that we meet in most ancient records and in primitive societies" ("Approaching," 83). Buck is such a natural symbol which establishes a link between the reader and his own unconscious. Reading the story of Buck is like having an archetypal dream in a state of wakefulness, and we respond to it on a deeply emotional level. Through him we recover the link we have lost with the natural world. Our scientific and mechanical environment has isolated us in the cosmos because we are no longer involved with natural phenomena or with our instinctual nature. Nature has no more mysteries; thunder is no longer the voice of an angry God; the forest is no longer populated with werewolves or bush souls; and we have lost the profound emotional energy which a close contact with nature gave primitive man. As for our instinctual nature, we tend to either deny its existence or consider its manifestations as "evil."

But Buck is a dog, and therefore moral values are irrelevant to him. Through his process of individuation we can live out our own individuation vicariously; we can experience our own aggressiveness and urge to kill, our desire to return to a simpler and more primitive way of life; recapture our link with nature and our instincts; discard the problems of civilization, moral duties and complexities; live out our own nature fully with no concerns for anything else, while our moral and censorious persona is held in abeyance. We could never accept him as fully if he were a human character because we can no longer accept consciously these aspects of our personality. We want to think of ourselves as "evolved," "civilized"; Buck is telling us that we still have in us, below the surface, the same primitive man who existed a few hundred thousand years ago.

8

Buck as Mythical Hero

Myth is both simple and complex, concrete and abstract.

> Speaking generally, a myth is a story—a symbolical fable as simple
> as it is striking—which sums up an infinite number of more or less
> analogous situations. A myth makes it possible to become aware
> at a glance of certain types of *constant relations* and to disengage
> these from the welter of everyday appearances. . . . It has fre-
> quently been noted that myths never have an author. The origin
> of a myth has to be *obscure*, and so to some extent has its mean-
> ing. A myth stands forth as the entirely anonymous expression of
> collective—or, more exactly common—facts. . . . *But the most
> profound characteristic of a myth is the power with which it wins
> us over, usually without our knowing*. If a story, an event, or some
> leading human figure may turn into a myth, it is precisely by
> virtue of coming to hold sway over us as though against our
> will. . . . The statement of a myth disarms all criticism, and rea-
> son, if not silenced, becomes at least ineffective.[1]

While Denis de Rougemont sees myth mainly as a social phenomenon,
the expression of the "*rules of conduct* of a given social or religious
group," one may see it more comprehensively as the expression of a

powerful human drive, a subconscious or unconscious drive or yearning which controls human behavior and over which reason holds no sway. Myths arise from man's experience of life but have been shaped by his unconscious.

Pioneers of the study of the human psyche recognized this implicitly when they used mythical figures to name some basic motivating instincts. Sigmund Freud called the boy's attraction to his mother and hostility to his father the Oedipus complex after the Greek myth of Oedipus, who killed his father and married his mother, and the girl's resentment of her mother and attachment to her father the Electra complex after the Greek myth of Electra, the daughter of Agamemnon, who avenged her father's death by destroying her mother and her lover (Clytemnestra and Aegisthus) who had murdered him. Similarly, the modern scientific concept of heredity was present in the Greek concept of Fate. The nineteenth and twentieth centuries have often redefined in scientific terms what preceding civilizations knew through empirical knowledge and had dramatized in myth and tragedies.

Myths have their origins in man's unconscious. Primordial human emotions, motivations, and actions are dramatized through myths that transcend any one interpretation and are always open to a variety of readings. Myths do not come to life as coherent systems, such as philosophies, theologies, or scientific theories, but grow at random, like weeds, in every civilization, and evolve with ethnic and historic conditions, each succeeding generation not necessarily requiring them to express the same truths. Very early, however, especially in the case of Greek myths, mythical figures became *real*, in the sense that they took on a vivid personality under the pen of great poets or dramatists, such as Homer, who created in the *Iliad* an unforgettable Achilles, the epitome of the warrior who chose a short but glorious life over a long and peaceful one. Even in Antiquity, the interpretations of myth varied. For instance, Aeschylus saw Prometheus as the universal redeemer, a powerful symbol of hope and idealism in his *Prometheus Bound*, while Hesiod saw him in desperate terms as having brought original sin to mankind and as having corrupted the human condition, a symbol of man's eternal separation from the divine. In the legend,

Oedipus was merely the representative of a cursed generation, a mere link in the unfolding of the catastrophes loosed upon the descendants of Laïos, but he became in Sophocles' *Oedipus Rex* an innocent victim of a cruel fate and, eventually, in *Oedipus Coloneus* a protective and beneficent hero through his suffering and acceptance of the will of the Gods. Modern playwrights and writers have also been fascinated by myths and shaped their personal interpretations of them. Racine's *Electre*, Eugene O'Neill's *Mourning Becomes Electra*, Jean Giraudoux's *Electre*, Jean Paul Sartre's *Les Mouches* (also a dramatization of the myth of Electra), Jean Cocteau's *La Machine infernale* (a dramatization of the myth of Oedipus), Albert Camus's *Le Mythe de Sisyphe*, and Shelley's "Prometheus Unbound" are but a few such interpretations that follow the main outline of each myth but dramatize it in different psychological terms.

The Call of the Wild dramatizes several myths that are as present in our modern society as they were in the societies preceding ours: the Myth of the Hero, the Myth of the Descent into Hell, initiation rituals, the passage into adulthood, the Son/Horde Myth, the Pastoral Myth, and the Myth of Love. Buck's journey into hell follows a traditional heroic pattern and involves rituals of passage and initiation into the "Heart of Darkness."

While the Myth of the Hero is perhaps the most common and best known, it cannot be defined in simple terms. There are many hero myths which vary greatly in detail, but which follow a more or less universal pattern. Joseph Campbell indicates in *The Hero with a Thousand Faces* that the role of the hero is to find regeneration within himself by retreating into the internal world of the self (the "everlasting realm that is within"), and to gain a "vivid renewal of life" by grasping all of the "life potentialities" that were never realized in his adulthood. By calling up from the depth of his unconscious strengths and knowledge that have been forgotten by his civilization, he can become a boon-bringer to his people; and, by reaching the archetypes that inspire myth, he presents a vision that is eternal because it comes "pristine from the primary springs of human life and thought . . . the unquenched source through which society is born."[2]

The adventure of the hero in myth follows a general pattern of separation, initiation, and return. The first stage of the separation is the call to adventure. It involves a rite or moment of passage that, when completed, amounts to a dying and rebirth, while familiar life horizons, old ideals, and emotional patterns are replaced by new ones. Characterizing the call to adventure are usually a dark forest and a terrifying herald who guides the hero toward "That which has to be faced, and is somehow profoundly familiar to the unconscious" but which is frightening to the conscious mind. What was formerly meaningful may suddenly become strangely empty of value. This initial call to adventure indicates that destiny has summoned the hero. If the hero responds to the call, he will usually meet a helper, a protective figure who indicates that a benign power is at his side and who can be seen as an initiatory priest, the personification of the hero's destiny, or merely as a guide who accompanies the hero to the first threshold, the entrance into a "zone of magnified power." This threshold is watched by a guardian who represents the limits of the hero's present sphere, beyond which stretch darkness, the unknown, and danger. "The adventure is always a passage beyond the veil of the known to the unknown; the powers that watch the boundaries are dangerous; to deal with them is risky; yet for someone with ability and courage, the danger fades."

Having passed the threshold, the hero moves into the second phase of the adventure/initiation. He "moves in a dream landscape of curiously fluid, ambiguous forms, where he must survive a succession of trials," and is aided either by an amulet or by the supernatural helper. After overcoming all the trials, he goes on to the ultimate adventure, the mystical marriage to the "queen-goddess of the world," which represents his mastery of life. But the hero further seeks spiritual revelation, which leads him to a stage that Campbell refers to as "atonement with the father," or "at-one-ment" (becoming one with the father). He is then reborn symbolically in that he himself becomes the father. Finally, the boon which the hero desires is an unending sustenance, food in either the physical sense (the feasting of heroes in Norse mythology) or in a spiritual sense. After gaining the boon, he must return, but he might refuse to do so. If he returns, he becomes the master of two worlds, with the ability to pass back and forth across the division from the world of time to timelessness.

This compendium of the major stages of the Myth of the Hero is taken from many different myths, no single myth following the complete outline, or events necessarily taking place in the same order, except in the largest sense. Joseph Campbell, in fact, uses different legends to illustrate different points.

Earle Labor recognized early that the story of Buck follows the basic pattern of the Myth of the Hero: "The call to adventure, departure, initiation, the perilous journey to the 'world navel' or mysterious life-center, transformation, and apotheosis . . . all are present in Buck's progress from the civilized world through the natural and beyond to the supernatural world" (*Jack*, 72). Labor sees the first three chapters of the novel as dramatizing the first stage of the myth. Chapter 1, "Into the Primitive," dramatizes the physical separation of Buck from his environment, a break not of Buck's choosing and one he resists with all his might. The man in the red sweater acts as the high priest of Buck's initiatory rites, mercilessly beating into him the new rules he will have to live by. Chapter 2, "The Law of Club and Fang," takes the hero to the North, where he meets the dogs he is going to live with and the men he will have to obey. This second stage of his initiation marks not only his physical but also his moral evolution: to survive he must become a different dog, and moral values that were meaningful to him in the past lose all meaning in a world where the only rule is: kill or be killed, eat or be eaten. According to Labor, chapter 3, "The Dominant Primordial Beast," marks the conclusion of the first major phase of Buck's initiation for it reveals that he is not merely qualified as a member of the pack but that he is also worthy of leadership. Indeed, Buck has now overcome Spitz who, like the man in the red sweater, had initiated him into the world of harsh survival, defeating in Spitz not only the lead dog of the team and a teacher but also active malevolence.

Although Buck has now "Won to Mastership," he is not yet ready for apotheosis. He still has to overcome several trials, the first of which climaxes in a symbolical, almost literal death. In chapter 5, "The

Toil of Trace and Trail," Buck has to survive man's ultimate and self-destructive stupidity, embodied in the three *chekakos*, Charles, his wife Mercedes, and her brother Hal. They overwork, starve, and beat the dogs; they are lazy, self-indulgent, and stupid; they lack foresight and never contemplate the logical consequences of their actions. They are, in fact, far more dangerous to the dogs and to themselves than intelligent malevolence as embodied in Spitz. Buck's experience with them climaxes with his being beaten almost to death and his acceptance of death rather than continued life under their rule.

Earle Labor sees John Thornton, who prevents Hal from killing Buck, as the benevolent helper of myth who traditionally appears to lead the hero toward his goal. There is much justification for this view, but Thornton is not only the benign helper who allows Buck to continue his journey, eventually becoming a God figure as well as a heroic one, but also the love goddess whom the hero must outgrow in order to come fully into his own. Thornton embodies for Buck the gifts of life and of love, which are traditionally and mythically associated with female archetypes, and plays the role of the life-giving and nurturing mother, while the man in the red sweater, François and Perrault, the "Scotch half-breed," and Spitz had all played the roles of father figures whom Buck had to live with, obey, learn from, and eventually, in the case of Spitz, defeat.

John Thornton is the ideal master:

> Other men saw to the welfare of their dogs from a sense of duty and business expediency; he saw to the welfare of his as if they were his own children, because he could not help it. And he saw further. He never forgot a kindly greeting or a cheering word, and to sit down for a long talk with them ("gas" he called it) was as much his delight as theirs. He had a way of taking Buck's head roughly between his hands, and resting his own head upon Buck's, of shaking him back and forth, the while calling him ill names that to Buck were love names. Buck knew no greater joy than that rough embrace and the sound of murmured oaths, and at each jerk back and forth it seemed that his heart would be shaken out of his body so great was its ecstasy. (108)

Thornton's care and kindness arouse in Buck's heart a great passion: "Love, genuine passionate love . . . love that was feverish and burning, that was adoration, that was madness" (108). Because of this great love, Buck is willing to give his life for Thornton, proving it on three major occasions, to Thornton's and his friends' awe. On the first occasion, Buck jumps over a cliff, "which fell away, straight down, to naked bed-rock three hundred feet below" (112), at Thornton's command, and it is only because Thornton, Hans, and Pete catch him and abort his jump that he does not crash down on the rock below. A few days later, Buck saves Thornton's life in the rapids, in a "stretch of wild water in which no swimmer could live" (114). Three times Buck goes out into the rapids at the risk of his own life to save Thornton's, succeeding on the third attempt:

> He was half drowned, and Hans and Pete threw themselves upon him, pounding the breath into him and the water out of him. He staggered to his feet and fell down. The faint sound of Thornton's voice came to them, and though they could not make out the words of it, they knew that he was in his extremity. His master's voice acted on Buck like an electric shock. He sprang to his feet and ran up the bank ahead of the men to the point of his previous departure. . . .
>
> . . . Strangling, suffocating, sometimes one uppermost and sometimes the other, dragging over the jagged bottom, smashing against rocks and snags, they veered in to the bank. (115)

After having been brought to, Buck finally escapes the ordeal with three broken ribs. A final, less heroic but perhaps more spectacular, instance of Buck's devotion is the scene in which he wins a bet for Thornton by breaking out of the ice and pulling for a hundred yards a sleigh loaded with a thousand pounds of flour to the raving admiration of a Dawson crowd. The spectators are awed by the communion existing between the man and the dog: "Thornton rose to his feet. His eyes were wet. The tears were streaming frankly down his cheeks. . . . Buck seized Thornton's hand in his teeth. Thornton shook him back and forth. As though animated by a common impulse, the onlookers drew back to a respectful distance; nor were they again indiscreet enough to interrupt" (121).

While it is indeed with Thornton's help that Buck enters the final leg of his journey, Thornton embodies the softening influence of civilization, of love, and of women and would eventually inhibit Buck's progression toward divinity should their relationship continue. This is why he must disappear if Buck is to fulfill his heroic destiny. Indeed, while Thornton is a guide, his very existence also restrains Buck from following his higher call: "He [Buck] was older than the days he had seen and the breaths he had drawn. He linked the past with the present, and the eternity behind him throbbed through him in a mighty rhythm to which he swayed as the tides and the seasons swayed. . . . Deep in the forest a call was sounding. . . . But as often as he gained the soft unbroken earth and the green shade, the love of John Thornton drew him back" (110–11).

Earle Labor rightly tells us that the landscape Thornton and his party enter in "The Sounding of the Call" is the landscape of myth, a zone unknown, the "fateful region of both treasure and danger" described by Joseph Campbell. It is a fabled lost mine that many men had sought, but few had found: "[A]nd more than a few there were who had never returned from the quest. This lost mine was steeped in tragedy and shrouded in mystery. . . . From the beginning there had been an ancient and ramshackle cabin. Dying men had sworn to it, and to the mine the site of which it marked, clinching their testimony with nuggets that were unlike any known grade of gold in the Northland" (122). This is indeed beyond the realm of the mundane. It is the final stage of the journey which only a few courageous men will undertake and from which only one hero chosen by the Gods will return. Described rather quickly in chapter 7, the journey takes in fact about a year and a half and is surrounded by an aura of timelessness—from the winter in Dawson when Buck wins $1,600 for Thornton, through spring, summer, and fall, then through a second winter and spring. Time, however, seems unimportant: "The months came and went, and back and forth they twisted through the uncharted vastness, where no men were and yet where men had been if the Lost Cabin were true. . . . In the fall of the year they penetrated a weird lake country, sad and silent, where wildfowl had been, but where then there was no life nor sign of life—only the blowing of chill winds, the forming of ice in sheltered places, and the melancholy rippling of waves on lonely beaches" (123–24).

The weirdness of the countryside they have entered suggests clearly that they are nearing the end of their journey, and that the final tests are to come. In this typical setting for ritual testing, nature seems to be holding its breath, waiting for the hero to come into his own. In fact, most of the significant tests Buck undergoes take place in *mandala*-like settings—usually the center of a circle. When he is beaten by the man in the red sweater, the confrontation takes place in a "small, high-walled back yard" with the four men who had brought him there sitting on top of the wall to watch the performance. When he witnesses the death of Curly and learns by proxy the "law of fang," he is part of the intent and silent circle surrounding the combatants. When he defeats Spitz, he and Spitz are at the center of that same silent and intent circle where the ritual of life and death is played out in traditional fashion, while time seems suspended and nature in abeyance: "He seemed to remember it all,—the white woods, and earth, and moonlight, and the thrill of battle. Over the whiteness and silence brooded a ghostly calm. There was not the faintest whisper of air—nothing moved, not a leaf quivered, the visible breath of the dogs rising slowly and lingeringly in the frosty air" (78). When Buck stands off the wolf pack after Thornton's death, he is standing "motionless as a statue" at the very center of a clearing in the forest "where the moonlight streamed" and the wolves "poured in a silvery flood" (137–38). This is his final test. After having defeated the Yeehats and thus put to rest the "law of club," he has now defeated the leader and best fighters of the wolf pack and not only earned entrance into the primeval world but achieved a position of leadership. He is now, indeed, the master of two worlds, and neither holds any fear for him.

In the strictest sense of Joseph Campbell's interpretation of the Myth of the Hero, the last stage of the myth is not fulfilled in that Buck does not return to the world of men and become a boon-bringer. Such a return would have been a fall from the superior godlike position he has achieved. There is no grandeur or glory in being a pampered pet, while there is grandeur in being a gloriously coated wolf running at the head of the pack and singing the song of a primeval world. Unlike Marlow or Kurtz in *Heart of Darkness*, Buck has found no horror during his trip into hell and has therefore no reason to return. Much to the contrary, he has been able to tap into an unknown source of power that had been buried for centuries and to find regeneration within himself by retreating into "the everlasting realm that is within." He has fulfilled all his latent potentialities and is at one with his inner yearning and the past of his breed. Buck's being an animal makes this identification easier to accept by human consciences. While Kurtz does essentially the same thing, he is racked by guilt and destroyed because his moral nature cannot cope with the things his instincts and desires force him to do. For Buck, there is no such dilemma.

However, a form of return and of boon-bringing does exist. While Buck does not return to the world of civilization, he returns to the world which is truly his—the world of the wild and of the wolves. He becomes more than ever a social being, since he becomes the leader of a highly socialized unit (the wolf pack) and to this social unit he is a boon-bringer, for he brings to them a knowledge of the world of men. Under his leadership, the wolf pack no longer fears man. On the contrary, it is the Yeehats who fear this Ghost Dog, "for it has cunning greater than they, stealing from their camps in fierce winters, robbing their traps, slaying their dogs, and defying their bravest hunters" (139). Buck is also a boon-bringer to the readers, for he makes them feel, even for a moment, the life potentialities inside themselves, the soaring primitive aspects of their unconscious, the transcendent, immortal life power that Campbell believes is buried in everyone. Buck is a life-giver in the wasteland of modern society.

While many critics recognize the presence of the Myth of the Hero in *The Call of the Wild*, they do not all agree on the various stages of Buck's initiation and apotheosis. Partly following in Maxwell Geismar's traces, Charles N. Watson, Jr., sees Buck's experiences mainly as a passage into adulthood and as a dramatization of the Son/Horde Myth described by J. G. Frazer in *The Golden Bough* and

053870

of Freud's argument in *Totem and Taboo*.[3] "According to such theories, the ritual sacrifice reenacts the primal parricide, in which a son, cast out of the horde by his father, returns at the head of a band of brothers to kill the father and usurp his leadership."[4] Both Geismar and Watson see the scene of Spitz and Buck's final confrontation as the culmination of the rites of sacrifice and of succession. While this is quite convincing, as Buck's whole adventure dramatizes his passage into adulthood, there is much more because the killing of Spitz forms merely one stage of Buck's evolution on his way to becoming not only a hero but also a God. Watson also sees Judge Miller's estate and the warm Southland as maternal and virtually womb symbols, Buck's abduction as his being orphaned, and his life with John Thornton as a temporary regression from adulthood into childhood dependency. Again, this cannot really be quarreled with, but there is more because Thornton plays a complex role in Buck's life and development. He is indeed at once a father figure, a mother figure, a lover figure, and a guide into the womb-of-time. Moreover, it is rather difficult to view Buck as a helpless dependent, since he is truly a partner with the men who rely on him as much as he relies on them. It is not an association of weaklings, but an association of strong, independent beings, self-reliant and self-assured. Watson's vision of Buck as a demonic figure is much less convincing and imposes a value judgment on an experience to which moral values are irrelevant because the hero of the story is an animal, not a human being. That human characters such as the man in the red sweater, François, and the Yeehats should refer to Buck as a devil within the novel, or that London himself should occasionally do so, is largely an instance of anthropomorphism.[5]

James Cooper finds that the Myth of the Hero provides the prevailing theme for *The Call of the Wild*,[6] but he sees Buck's initiatory journey as ending when he lands in Dyea Beach. During this initiatory journey, which he variously defines as a journey "into the dark interior of the collective unconscious and the womb," as "the conscious mind's first encounter with the unconscious and the dark forces that lie hidden there," and, symbolically, as "an entry into the dark waters of the womb to which the fetus must learn to accommodate itself before it begins to grow towards rebirth," Buck encounters people, such as the man in the red sweater, who instruct him in ways to survive. From Dyea Beach on, Cooper sees Buck as being adopted by a series of human foster parents and as being "suckled by the dogs" who teach him the ways of his new environment. His education is seen as a series of vacillations between horror and ecstasy before he reaches the final summit during the pursuit of the rabbit. The picture of Buck's being suckled by the dogs as Remus and Romulus were by the wolves is inappropriate, since Buck is far from being a helpless puppy. This interpretation also disrupts the sequence of the Myth of the Hero rather unconvincingly, for Buck's learning to steal, his sly encouragement to the other dogs to defy Spitz's authority, his glorying in the kill, fit Cooper's definition of the initiatory journey as the mind's first encounter with its dark side and its gradual acceptance of these dark forces far better than the single episode of the man in the red sweater.

Cooper also sees the pursuit of the rabbit and its shriek, "the cry of Life plunging down from Life's apex in the grip of Death," as a description of Buck's own plunging down from the summit (the summit of life being in fact a prelude to death), and, more importantly, as an admittance into the "real" world as opposed to the dream world of the womb. According to Cooper, Buck's killing of the bull moose is the blood sacrifice necessary for his becoming a hero. Again, this is not entirely convincing for, if sacrifice there is, it is on the part of the other moose who accept to pay the toll to save the herd from Buck's threatening presence, and, in this way, propitiate this God of the Wild so that the herd might move on. What Cooper does not see is that if Buck makes a blood sacrifice, although unknowingly and certainly unwillingly, it is that of John Thornton's life. Thornton is indeed sacrificed to Buck's increasing desire to follow the call. Had he renounced his primal side and stayed with Thornton, Buck would have been able to save him, as evidenced by his subsequent dealings with the Yeehats. In fact, the sacrifice of Thornton fits in far better with the Son/Horde Myth, for Buck has now not only slayed his bad father in the shape of Spitz but also, indirectly, his good one.

Cooper sees Buck's encounter with the old, gaunt, and battle-scarred wolf (138) as coming face to face with his true spiritual father. Choosing the old wolf as Buck's spiritual father seems rather gratuitous, for the only thing the old wolf does that might qualify him is break out into the long wolf howl, which is then picked up by the rest of the pack—a song Buck joins, now recognizing the unmistakable accents of the call (138–39). The first wolf Buck encounters in the forest would seem a better spiritual father because he becomes Buck's first real link with his forefathers (126–28). It is while running with this first wolf that Buck first realizes that he is at last answering the call, "running by the side of his wood brother toward the place from where the call surely came" (128). This wolf is also the first to make friendly overtures after Buck has stood off the pack. The old wolf is probably not even the leader of the pack and, therefore, cannot qualify as the father whom Buck has to wrestle for leadership. The leader was probably, according to wolf custom, the first to attack Buck and the one whose neck Buck broke.

Finally, James Cooper's interpretation seems to overlook about a third of the book, jumping from the killing of the rabbit to the "blood sacrifice" of the moose. Thus, a major part of the novel is not integrated within his argument, which weakens his claim that the Myth of the Hero provides the prevailing theme of the story.

In her article, "The Wolf and the Mirror," Ann Upton, relying in part on Norse mythology, sees the wolf as both a destroyer and a preserver and claims that London uses the symbol of the wolf to explore his own nature; by identifying with "an animal that looks the same in both wild and domesticated states [he] vicariously journey[s] from domestication into the primitive and back again."[7] She also sees Buck as the archetypal hero of Campbell's work. However, for her, Buck's call to adventure comes when he hears the cry of the wolf in Thornton's camp, and his journey from the common world into a region of supernatural wonder comes when he dashes through the woods after the cry. He encounters fabulous forces when he meets the timber wolf, and his decisive victory comes when he defeats the wolves and gains entry into the wolf pack. The problem with Upton's analysis is that she ignores eight-tenths of the novel: chapters 1 to 6 inclusive.

The Myth of the Hero, indeed, informs the story throughout, and no significant portion of the novel falls outside of it. While *The Call of the Wild* may not follow in every respect Campbell's ideal and synthesized stages of the myth, it nevertheless dramatizes all its major stages from chapter 1 to 7, from initial departure to final and inspiring godlike state.

The other major myth which informs the novel is the Pastoral Myth. Although less overwhelmingly so than the Myth of the Hero, it is a vital part of the story. Indeed, the novel vividly dramatizes man's desire to escape from the complexities of an artificial civilization to the simplicity of nature, conveying London's revulsion from modern life and society and expressing his need to escape to "naked and howling savagery" in a natural jungle, which, by comparison with an urban and human one, seems refreshing and cleansing.

The Pastoral Myth has been shared by most advanced civilizations as far back as the Roman Empire and earlier and has been a constant in American literature. It was, however, sorely thwarted by the closing of the Frontier. Suddenly there was no more empty space to escape to when one felt dissatisfied, and Californian writers seemed particularly sensitive to the disappearance of open spaces, since they were born on the Last Frontier of the American continent. Raymond Benoit sees *The Call of the Wild* as a "ritual enactment of the American wish to turn back to simplicity": "[T]he myth of Buck, the great dog, is an embodiment of the American Dream of escaping from the entangling complexity of modern living back to a state as unencumbered as the sled that Buck pulls. Buck, from this angle, is as much an American hero as Rip Van Winkle—he shakes superfluities from himself."[8] Indeed, the question of the return to simplicity "reverberates with the force of an archetype" throughout American literature. After all, people came to America from the very beginning to get away from everything they had been and had known, and they kept on getting away, pushing westward after settling the East Coast and the prairies until California was reached and settled. It is thus logical that getting away should be a major theme in American literature, from Hector St. Jean de Crèvecoeur, James Fenimore Cooper's Leatherstocking tales, Thoreau's *Walden*, experiments such as Brook Farm and the like, Whitman's *Leaves of Grass*, through to Sherwood Anderson, who lamented that a kind of beautiful childlike innocence had gone forever, Sinclair Lewis, Ernest Hemingway, John Steinbeck, William

Faulkner, and contemporary American poets. All sang the beauties of a simple life in the heart of nature. That they actually never followed their own preaching, or only for a short time, made the American Dream even more powerful in that it was never seriously confronted with actuality and thus remained wishful thinking.

Benoit also mentions the two types of heroes who haunt American life and literature: the "Franklins" on the one hand, and the "Thoreaus" on the other—those who get ahead and those who live in harmony with nature and dance to their own tune instead of to the tune of the world. In *The Call of the Wild*, three men exemplify the Thoreau ideal: Buck's last masters—Thornton, Hans, and Pete. They are men who live "close to the earth, thinking simply and seeing clearly" (111). Asking little of man and nature, they are unafraid of the wild. "With a handful of salt and a rifle [Thornton] could plunge into the wilderness and fare wherever he pleased and as long as he pleased. Being in no haste, Indian fashion, he hunted his dinner in the course of the day's travel; and if he failed to find it, like the Indian, he kept on traveling, secure in the knowledge that sooner or later he would come to it" (123). These men are Nature's Noblemen. Buck himself seems to be both types of heroes at the same time. He certainly gets ahead by achieving the leadership of the dog team, then the leadership of the wolf pack, but he does so by dancing to his own tune and living in perfect harmony with both nature and his deeper self, thus conciliating in his furry person both types of American heroes and healing the split in the divided American consciousness.

If the Franklins are not really dramatized in the book, although Benoit sees them in Spitz, the cold and calculating lead dog, their antitheses are certainly dramatized in Hal, Charles, and Mercedes, who want to get ahead but have none of the virtues that Benjamin Franklin felt were necessary to succeed: temperance, silence, order, resolution, frugality, industry, sincerity, justice, moderation, cleanliness, tranquility, chastity, and humility. In fact, the trio appears as a caricature of the archetype of the successful American. They are self-indulgent, noisy (they never stop complaining and quarreling), cowardly, lazy, unjust, selfish, resentful, sloppy, disorganized, and convinced they know all. They embody in most respects the worst that society has to offer, and their messy sled, which tips over because it is overloaded with needless apparatus, symbolizes the burden of civilization on modern man. It is the weight of their own baggage and stupidity that cracks the ice and brings about their demise, and it is London's warning for the world of the twentieth century.

Several critics have mentioned that *The Call of the Wild* is an archetypally American book because of its criticism of society. Indeed, few literatures have been as critical of the society which gave them rise as American literature. The greater the dream, the greater the disappointment. The novel has also been compared to *The Adventures of Huckleberry Finn* and to *Moby-Dick*, both of which are also escape classics. But *The Call of the Wild* is more simple, more elemental, and requires no knowledge of American life to be fully understood. Buck is also an archetypal American hero, and one might describe him as a dog who turns his back on society. A dog who keeps his moral integrity hard and intact. An isolate, almost selfless, stoic, enduring dog, who lives by death, by killing, but who is pure white.[9] Clearly Buck is not white in coat, but he is "white" inside, where it counts—that is, he is just, pure, and innocent. However, unlike the traditional American hero, from Deerslayer on, Buck can "marry" and have offspring without falling from his elevated stature—that, too, is his dog's privilege.

9

A Romantic Novel

A naturalistic, a mythical, and an archetypal novel, *The Call of the Wild* is also a romantic novel. *Romantic*, however, is a term that is and has been used in many different ways. The epithets *romantic* and *classic* have traditionally been used as opposites, the latter being associated with the concept of equilibrium and the first with lack or interruption of equilibrium. However, there is no real conflict because both denote moments of the human spirit—order naturally following upon disorder or chaos. According to Paul Valéry, "*Tout classicisme suppose un romantisme antérieur.*" "Le classique implique donc des actes volontaires et réfléchis qui modifient une production 'naturelle' conformément à une conception *claire et rationnelle* de l'homme et de l'art." (Any form of classicism presupposes a former romanticism. The production of a classical work implies the modification by a process both conscious and willed of a 'spontaneous' production according to a clear and rational concept of man and art.)[1] Paul Valéry is thus contrasting emotions and inspiration on the one hand with reasoned action and craftsmanship on the other, the first being characteristic of Romanticism and the second of Classicism, with Classicism naturally becoming a secondary stage of Romanticism. As Mario Praz indicates in *The Romantic Agony*: "It is not the content which decides whether a work should be labelled 'romantic' or not, but the spirit. . . . There is no opposite pole to 'romantic,' merely because 'romantic' indicates a certain state of sensibility which, simply, is different from any other, and not comparable either by coordination or by contrast."[2]

The word *romantic* appears for the first time in English in the midseventeenth century, meaning "like the old romances," in an attempt to give a name to certain characteristics of the chivalrous and pastoral romances. However, the characteristics referred to by the adjective *romantic* were generally negative, indicating mostly the falsity, the unreality, the fantastic and irrational nature of the events and sentiments dramatized in these romances. People spoke of romantic exaggeration and romantic absurdities. At the beginning of the eighteenth century the word took on more positive connotations and took on the flavor of "attractive" and pleasing to the imagination, but still slightly absurd. *Romantic* also came to be used to describe landscapes similar to those described in romances, but without any note of scorn. Gradually the word lost its connection with the literary genre from which it was originally derived and came to express love for the wild and melancholy aspects of nature.

In the last quarter of the eighteenth century, French writers came to differentiate between *romanesque, pittoresque,* and *romantique.* They thought of *romanesque* as meaning chimerical or fabulous; *pittoresque* was used to describe a scene that strikes the eye and arouses admiration; and *romantique* came to be used not only to describe a scene or scenery, but also the emotion aroused in the person viewing it. *Romantique* thus assumed a subjective character, describing not only the object but also our reaction to it. In 1929 M. Deutschbein, in his essay on "Romantish und Romanesk," tried to differentiate the two concepts. He felt that *Romanesk* should be used to designate the exotic, the strange, or the grotesque, while *Romantish* should be used for genuine Romanticism, whose essence, according to him, lies in a deep understanding of the harmony of the universe. In 1926 Lascelles Abercrombie shared a similar point of view and felt that one of the most important characteristics of Romanticism consists in a retreat from the external world to an "inner" world, a withdrawal from outer things into inner experience, as opposed to Realism, which goes out into the real world. For Abercrombie *Romanticism* was identified with the inner urge of artistic inspiration.

Although Romanticism and Realism are traditionally seen as being at odds, there is no fundamental incompatibility. Emile Zola started out as a Romantic before espousing Realism and going a step further into Naturalism. Other French Realists, such as Gustave Flaubert, followed a similar progression, and an American Realist like Frank Norris claimed in "The Responsibilities of the Novelist" that Naturalism is but a form of Romanticism. Norris saw Realism as the commonplace tale of commonplace people, best exemplified in the novels of William Dean Howells. Revolting against this approach, he felt that literature should dramatize the "unplumbed depths of the human heart," the mystery of sex, the problems of life, and "the black unsearched penetralia of the soul of man."[3] In his eyes, only Romance could chronicle this type of life and handle its sordid elements, which he felt Zola had done. Thus, for Norris, Naturalism, Zolaism, and Romance were intimately linked. According to him, Howells's characters live across the street from the reader while Zola's characters live in a world of their own: "Terrible things must happen to the characters of the naturalistic tale. They must be twisted from the ordinary, wrenched out from the quiet, uneventful round of every-day life, and flung into the throes of a vast terrible drama that works itself out in unleashed passions, in blood and in sudden death. The world of Mr. Zola is a world of big things; the enormous, the formidable, the terrible is what counts. No teacup tragedies here."[4] Although it unfairly belittles Howells's novels as "tea-cup tragedies," this description of Naturalism establishes clearly the link with Romanticism. Many romantic tragedies could be described in exactly the same terms. Indeed, tragical and mythical heroes are also great romantic figures, and there is more romance in being an Achilles, living a short and glorious life and dying in battle, than in being an old man (or woman) dying in bed after a long and dull, if reasonably happy, existence.

Irving Babbitt in *Rousseau and Romanticism* sees no fundamental change of direction between Romanticism and Realism and feels that the two are bound together by their "common repudiation of decorum as something external and artificial. . . . At the bottom of much so-called realism . . . is a special type of satire, a satire that is the product of violent emotional disillusion."[5] Neither Zola nor London would have quarreled with this; both were born with a romantic sensibility, intense emotions, and a passionate love of justice and beauty. Their subsequent Naturalism was their way of protesting against the superficiality and hypocrisy of the many and against the ugliness of much of life. Thus Realism and its more extreme version, Naturalism, become a way of expressing in logical form a vibrant and frustrated romantic sensibility. By describing in detail the opposite of what is traditionally seen as romantic, one creates another form of Romanticism in two ways: the ugly suggesting by contrast the beautiful, and the ugly becoming romantic in itself because it arouses violent emotions.

Romantic assumes a subjective character which describes not so much the property of the object as our reaction to it. Something romantic is, according to Jean Paul in *Magie der Einbildungskraft* (Magic of the Imagination), something that exists only in aspiration and in remembrance. Things that are remote, dead, or unknown possess this transfiguring charm because imagination possesses the magic virtue of making things infinite. Indeed, the quality of romanticism exists not in the thing itself but in the eye of the beholder. A romantic book, a romantic scenery, a romantic experience, arouse deep and satisfying emotions. Thus, the essence of Romanticism cannot easily be described: it is that which reaches deep inside of us and brings to the fore emotions, desires, dreams, or yearnings. A Jungian might say that it is that which appeals to our unconscious.

It is therefore hardly surprising that *The Call of the Wild* should be one of the world's most romantic novels. Its naturalistic, mythical, and archetypal characteristics, far from being at odds with its romanticism, are an intrinsic part of it. But it is also romantic in other ways. Like much of London's work, it is romantic because of its emphasis on love, beauty, and justice, and because of its appeal to a complete range of emotions, from pity and anger to admiration and envy. It is also romantic because it dramatizes a human dream of adventure, freedom, and personal fulfillment—a dream which a depressed London felt was a hopeless one for himself and for much of humanity.

In writing about Jack London and Upton Sinclair, Alfred Kazin remarked that "the curious thing about these leading Socialist 'fiction-eers' is that they were the most romantic novelists of their times."[6] Indeed, London always wanted to "grasp the true Romance of things" and felt that, rightly considered, Romance should be true to Life and not shy away from grim Realities. In fact, he made it clear that, to be great, a story must deal with the tragic or terrible, and that fear is the most primordial emotion of all—it is the stirring of the savage in us, "of the savage who has slept, but never died, since the time the river-folk crouched over the fires of their squatting places, or the tree-folk bunched together and chattered in the dark."[7] Fear thus becomes romantic because it brings to the fore forgotten and repressed emotions. At the same time, London felt that courage was the great roman-tic emotion of the nobility which allowed one to act as if fear were not present and, by implication, to deny its existence. Although one always tends to think of love as the great romantic emotion, London points out that the great stories of the world seem all to depend upon the tragic and terrible for their strength and greatness. "Not half of them deal with love at all; and when they do, they derive their greatness, not from the love itself, but from the tragic and terrible with which the love is involved." Indeed, Romeo and Juliet are not remembered because their love slipped along smoothly. The tragic and terrible are romantic because they take us away from "the sweet commonplaces of life [which cannot] be made into anything else but sweet commonplace stories."

The Call of the Wild is certainly not a sweet commonplace story. It is a story that deals with passionate love—not romantic love, but love that arises from the depth of the self. There is, of course, the great love that Buck bears for John Thornton, which he proves on several occasions by his willingness to give his life for that of his master. His devotion is splendid and terrible. When he defends Thornton against "Black" Burton, he certainly plays the role of the knight at arms defending his Lord and Master, and his love is measured by his rage at Thornton's death, when he throws all caution to the wind and attacks man—man whom he had learned to fear above all: "For the last time in his life he allowed passion to usurp cunning and reason, and it was because of his great love for John Thornton that he lost his head. . . . Buck, a live hurricane of fury, hurl[ed] himself upon them [the Yeehats], in a frenzy to destroy. . . . There was no withstanding him. He plunged about in their very midst, tearing, rending, destroying, in constant and terrific motion which defied the arrows they discharged at him" (135–36). Thornton's death leaves a great void in Buck— "somewhat akin to hunger, but a void which ached and ached, and which food could not fill" (137).

There is also the remarkable love of trace and trail which grips all the dogs but is best exemplified by Dave. Dave's love of work and his relentless will to live on his own terms, doing what he loves, arouses pity for his suffering but admiration for his uncompromising passion:

> Sometimes, in the traces, when jerked by a sudden stoppage of the sled, or by straining to start it, he would cry out with pain. The drivers examined him but could find nothing. . . . Something was wrong inside, but they could locate no broken bones, could not make it out.
>
> . . . Sick as he was, Dave resented being taken out, grunting and growling while the traces were unfastened, and whimpering brokenheartedly when he saw Sol-leks in the position he had held and served so long. For the pride of trace and trail was his, and, sick unto death, he could not bear that another dog should do his work. (88)

Despite the pain, Dave will not give up his role as a sled-dog when he is taken out of the traces, running along the sled in the soft snow, instead of behind where the going was easy, and earning the respect of the dog drivers who eventually put him back in the traces, deeming it "a mercy, since Dave was to die anyway, that he should die in the traces, heart-easy and content" (89). Dave behaves very much like Manuel Garcia in Ernest Hemingway's "The Undefeated"—one of Hemingway's undisputed code heroes—who will fight bulls to the end, although he no longer has the strength or the talent to do so successfully, and, even on his death bed, will not let his friends cut off his *coleta*, the symbol of his vocation. Primo Levi sees this passion of the dogs for their work as a "last refuge," an "alternative to servitude," and compares it to the wall gladly built by prisoners "struggling against the freezing cold of another arctic" in Solzhenitsyn's *One Day in the Life of Ivan Denisovitch*. This is work as a "form of intoxication," and, if it were not too human, one might almost say work as a last stand against the meaninglessness and pain of life. Amusingly, Primo Levi also sees Dave's brokenheartedness as representative of the human pathology of early retirement.[8]

Aside from love, two other powerful emotions inform the book: hatred and exaltation. Buck's bitter and deathless hatred of Spitz is aroused after the killing of Curly. However, Buck bides his time, waiting until he is ready and can win a fight which can only be to the death: "He was not prone to harshness and precipitate action, and in the bitter hatred between him and Spitz he betrayed no impatience, shunned all offensive acts" (65). Spitz's own hatred of Buck comes from his fear and his lack of understanding of Buck. He feels his supremacy threatened by Buck—this strange Southland dog who prospered while other Southland dogs "were all too soft, dying under the toil, the frost, and starvation" (35), and who matched him in strength, savagery, and cunning.

Even more powerful than love and hatred is the exaltation that Buck experiences at being alive in the face of death and which climaxes during the pursuit of the rabbit. It is an exaltation that seems to be shared by the whole of nature when it comes back to life in the spring:

> The ghostly winter silence had given way to the great spring murmur of awakening life. This murmur arose from all the land, fraught with the joy of living. It came to the things that lived and moved again, things which had been dead and which had not moved during the long months of frost. The sap was rising in the pines. The willows and aspens were bursting out in young buds. . . . Crickets sang in the nights, and in the days all manner of creeping, crawling things rustled forth into the sun. Partridges and woodpeckers were booming and knocking in the forest. Squirrels were chattering, birds singing, and overhead honked the

wild-fowl driving up from the south in cunning wedges that split the air. (103)

In fact, the book is a hymn to life and survival: to life that is defiant, full and rampant; to life that survives the worst trials and sufferings; to life that holds death and the White Silence at bay. London vividly describes time and again the forces of life and death that pull in opposite directions at all living creatures. His description of the frozen Northland at the beginning of *White Fang* is a classic:

> A vast silence reigned over the land. The land itself was a desolation, lifeless, without movement, so lone and cold that the spirit of it was not even that of sadness. There was a hint in it of laughter, but of a laughter more terrible than any sadness—a laughter that was mirthless as the smile of the Sphinx, a laughter cold as the frost and partaking of the grimness of infallibility. It was the masterful and incommunicable wisdom of eternity laughing at the futility of life and the effort of life. It was the Wild, the savage, frozen-hearted Northland Wild. (169)

Life which can survive for a time against such overwhelming odds has indeed a right to feel ecstatic pride in itself.

Although not human, Buck is a romantic hero. Not only does he possess great romantic qualities such as courage, endurance, leadership, loyalty, a passionate ability to love, and a total disregard of danger in defending or avenging those he loves, but he is also gorgeous. Physical beauty in itself has great romantic appeal, and romantic heroes or heroines are seldom ugly or merely plain. Moreover, we always tend to associate physical beauty with moral beauty, and the fact that there is no relationship of cause and effect between the two does not deter us. Indeed, we are naturally attracted to physical beauty, and a handsome Satan makes Evil seem more attractive than an old and deformed one.

London emphasizes time and again Buck's beauty, in particular in the last chapters. When Buck is about to pull a sled loaded with a thousand pounds of flour for the love of John Thornton, he is described as being

. . . in perfect condition, without an ounce of superfluous flesh, and in the one hundred and fifty pounds that he weighed were so many pounds of grit and virility. His furry coat shone with the sheen of silk. Down the neck and across the shoulders, his mane, in repose as it was, half bristled and seemed to lift with every movement, as though excess of vigor made each particular hair alive and active. The great breast and heavy forelegs were no more than in proportion with the rest of the body, where the muscles showed in tight rolls underneath the skin. Men felt these muscles and proclaimed them hard as iron. . . (118–19)

It is indeed difficult not to feel a thrill of admiration for such a gorgeous animal who seems to be the embodiment of natural strength and virility, as well as an animal one wants to cuddle because of his beautiful, soft, furry coat. The contrast between the powerful and iron-hard muscles that show through the silky, feminine coat is remarkably sensual and combines effectively the opposite attractions of the masculine and the feminine. Buck's short-lived moments of vulnerability are amusing but also remind us of his feminine side: his popping out of his first sleeping hole in sheer terror and, more importantly, his lying on his back, his four feet in the air, waiting for François to put on his sore feet the little moccasins he has manufactured for him. Even the most masculine and aggressive heroes, in London's work, are androgynous, and there is little doubt that Buck's appeal partakes of both the masculine and the feminine.[9]

Buck's physical beauty takes on a further glow when he begins to revert to the wild:

[He] became possessed of a great pride in himself, which communicated itself like a contagion to his physical being. It advertised itself in all his movements, was apparent in the play of every muscle, spoke plainly as speech in the way he carried himself, and made his glorious furry coat if anything more glorious.

. . . A carnivorous animal, living on a straight meat diet, he was in full flower, at the high tide of his life, overspilling with vigor and virility. . . . His muscles were surcharged with vitality, and snapped into play sharply, like steel springs. Life streamed through him in splendid flood, glad and rampant, until it seemed that it would burst him asunder in sheer ecstasy and pour forth generously over the world. (129–30)

Buck thus takes on the added attraction and mystery of the wild. He is all beauty and strength, but he also has the fascination of danger. Predators are always more romantic than their prey. Even with physical beauty and grace on both sides, the tiger is more romantic than the antelope, because our admiration for his beauty and the coordination of his movements is allied to our fear of the danger he represents, while our admiration for the beauty of the antelope is allied to our pity for its obvious fate. Because it distances emotionally from its object and demeans it, pity is not a romantic emotion. We want to be the tiger, not the antelope, the winner, not the vanquished. The tiger is therefore more pleasing to our imagination and our unconscious because our admiration is allied to the desire to be like him. Spontaneous identification with the antelope would suggest a death wish that would not be beneficial for the long-term survival of our own kind. As a gloriously successful and handsome predator Buck therefore embodies a natural instinct for survival. He is the life force that defies the White Silence, and, as such, he is eminently romantic.

In a 1915 letter, London described himself as "an idealist who believes in reality, and who, therefore, in all [he] write[s] strive[s] to be *real*, to keep both [his] feet and the feet of [his] readers on the ground so that no matter how high [they] dream [their] dreams will be based on reality."[10] The world he created in his work is also to some extent an ideal world where men, women, and dogs walk taller, and where they are more beautiful both physically and morally. It is also a world where a form of immanent justice prevails, which is very satisfying both intellectually and emotionally.

The justice that informs London's work usually takes the form of an essentially just working out of natural laws. In "In a Far Country," for instance, the two self-indulgent shirks and chronic grumblers, Weatherbee and Cuthfert, abandon their party and hole up in a lost cabin in the middle of the winter to avoid the pain of the trail, meeting a frightful end, starved and at each other's throats. There is nothing mysterious about their deaths, which are merely the logical consequence of their lack of self-discipline. They overeat, thus depleting needlessly their stock of food; their laziness turns into sloppiness, and neither will do any work; they distrust each other and, instead of cooperating, spend their time spying on each other. "Instead of being drawn together by their misery, each gloated over the other's symptoms as the scurvy took its course."[11] Eventually, they become paranoid and butcher each other. London's study of their psychology is relentless, and they are shown to be in every way the artisans of their own end. Similarly, the death of the man in "To Build a Fire" is perfectly logical in that he pays for his stupidity and vanity. Thinking he knows better than everyone else, although he is but a newcomer in the North, he attempts to travel alone with an outside temperature colder than 50 degrees below zero. After having broken through the ice and frozen his feet, and after having attempted to make a fire below a tree laden with snow, with the obvious taking place, he eventually freezes to death, realizing that the old-timer, who had told him that no one should travel alone in the Klondike after 50 degrees below zero, had been right.

Justice, at other times, may manifest itself as random chance, with no particular logic or inevitability. In "The White Silence," the great towering pine that crashes to the ground happens to crash down upon Mason who has just been guilty of deliberate cruelty in whipping viciously an already dying sled-dog. It is merely an accident of the trail. Trees laden with years will fall. But it is more satisfying to moral judgment that it should fall on Mason rather than on the Malemute Kid who tried to prevent Mason's gratuitous cruelty. Similarly, in "Where the Trail Forks," the three men who refuse to follow the code of the white man's honor and save the life of a young Indian girl because it might delay their return to California never do return. It is indeed poetic justice. In London's stories of the North, man may be destroyed if he makes errors or if he does not abide by the Northland code of honor that requires him to be courageous and enduring, adaptable and imaginative, unselfish and tolerant; he may be destroyed by his own unworthiness and greed; he may die simply because people do starve and freeze to death in such an environment; he may accomplish heroic deeds for no reward, except that the heroic deed becomes its own reward if accomplished for an honorable reason. A reward for heroism is not always dealt out by an unforgiving environment, but a punishment for the lack of it always is.

Both forms of justice are present in *The Call of the Wild*. The deaths of Hal, Charles, and Mercedes when the ice gives way under the weight of their sled and they disappear in a yawning hole is certainly a fit punishment for their cruelty toward the dogs whom they starved and overworked to death rather than let go of their own self-indulgent ways. Mercedes, in particular, refused to walk and, instead, rode on the sled, thus adding a lusty 120 pounds to the load the weak, starving, and abused dogs had to drag. Throughout the journey they are callous to the suffering of the animals, and their own incompetence and stubborn refusal to learn and mend their ways ensure their slow progress and the deaths of several of the dogs. While it serves a moral purpose, their punishment is nothing but the logical consequence of their actions. Like the man in "To Build a Fire," they disregard every principle of travel in the North and are the artisans of their own fate. That the remaining dogs should die with them, with the exception of Buck, is pitiful, but evidences another unpleasant fact of life: the irresponsible always seem to drag down with them innocent victims.

Another instance of immanent justice is the outcome of the fight between Buck and Spitz, the outcome of which is less obvious on a purely logical basis because the two opponents are evenly matched. However, London clearly intimates that it is Buck's superior ability that decides the outcome of the fight—less his physical strength, which is marginally superior to Spitz's since he is heavier, or his fighting technique, which is inferior to Spitz's, than his superior intelligence, or rather his superior imagination: "But Buck possessed a quality that made for greatness—imagination. He fought by instinct, but he could fight by head as well. He rushed, as though attempting the old shoulder trick, but at the last instant swept low to the snow and in. His teeth closed on Spitz's left foreleg. There was a crunch of breaking bone, and the white dog faced him on three legs" (79). Imagination is a necessity in London's world for his characters to survive. The man in "To Build a Fire" dies because of his arrogance but also, and, perhaps more importantly, because of his lack of imagination.

He was quick and alert in the things of life, but only in the things, and not in the significance. Fifty degrees below zero meant eighty odd degrees of frost. Such a fact impressed him as being cold and uncomfortable, and that was all. It did not lead him to meditate upon his frailty as a creature of temperature, and upon man's frailty in general, able only to live within certain narrow limits of heat and cold; . . . Fifty degrees below zero was to him just precisely fifty degrees below zero. That there should be anything more to it than that was a thought that never entered his head.[12]

This is where Buck's superior status really lies: he can outwit his enemy. His victory, moreover, serves a definite moral purpose.

While Buck is no angel, he has a streak of integrity and pride. He will obey the man in the red sweater, but he will not conciliate him. Even though he loves John Thornton passionately, he will not fawn upon him the way Skeet and Nig do. When Buck steals, he does so from sheer necessity and does not enjoy doing it. And when he systematically saps Spitz's authority over the team, he does so with a very precise aim in mind, not out of pure mischief—although there is no doubt that he enjoys it, swaggering under Spitz's nose while thwarting his punishment of offending dogs. It is, after all, war between the two dogs, both of whom intend to win that war at all costs. While Buck is not entirely innocent, Spitz has all the makings of a villain, if a handsome and courageous one. Spitz clearly enjoys the massacre of Curly, whose only sin was to be too trusting (56). Moreover, Spitz is inherently treacherous, ingratiating himself in a friendly way while meditating some underhand trick, as when he steals from Buck's food at the first meal (53). Once Spitz begins to feel threatened by Buck, he stops at nothing to get rid of his rival, from minor incidents, such as stealing his nest (66), to attacking him treacherously while Buck is fighting an enemy, as Spitz himself should be doing. Taking advantage of a generalized battle, Spitz prefers to attack his own side in the shape of Buck: "He [Buck] flung himself upon another [starving husky], and at the same time felt teeth sink into his own throat. It was Spitz, treacherously attacking from the side" (67). Spitz attacks Buck again when Buck is at a disadvantage after having run himself into exhaustion to avoid mad Dolly. "Buck staggered over against the sled, exhausted, sobbing for breath, helpless. This was Spitz's opportunity. He sprang upon Buck, and twice his teeth sank into his unresisting foe and ripped and tore the flesh to the bone. Then François's lash descended, and Buck had the satisfaction of watching Spitz receive the worst whipping as yet administered to any of the team" (71). It is therefore ethically satisfying to see Buck win the final contest against Spitz who possesses neither honor nor integrity. The "White Knight" does win against the "Black Knight," as in all good romantic tales; but, amusingly, the one with the white coat is Spitz, in a reversal of traditional attire.

The Call of the Wild is indeed a very romantic book, and Buck is a romantic hero. Despite his thick coat of fur, and perhaps because of it, the reader identifies with him easily and dreams through him of a world that is more beautiful, more just, and more exhilarating. Despite the presence throughout of death and suffering, *The Call of the Wild* is also essentially a positive book in that it offers a positive and meaningful vision of life. There is nothing absurd or revolting in this book where everything makes sense in realistic, psychological, and mythical terms. In it, London created a world vibrantly alive, which goes beyond the superficial niceties of existence to touch the roots of life, the primordial emotions that are firmly seated in all men. He also captured the true Romance of the North, white, pure, frozen, and utterly fascinating, of those who venture into it, and of the creatures who inhabit it. London's passionate love of life also permeates the book and communicates itself to even the most jaded reader. The intensity of the atmosphere never lets up and never allows the reader a moment's respite, except for the few instances of humor that remind us that Buck is after all a dog.

Notes and References

1. Social Context

1. Earle Labor, *Jack London* (New York: Twayne Publishers, 1974), 19; hereafter cited as *Jack*.

2. Joan London, *Jack London and His Times* (Seattle: University of Washington Press, 1968), 171; hereafter cited as *Times*.

3. Upton Sinclair, *The Jungle* (New York: Doubleday, Page, 1906).

4. See Ernest Untermann's letter to Joan London, 8 April 1938, Huntington Library, San Marino, Calif. Untermann was a fellow Socialist and close friend of London's who attempted to explain London's socialist beliefs to Joan, who was researching her father's life for her book *Jack London and His Times*. Two other letters dated 11 and 22 January 1938 are important in that respect. Unfortunately, Joan London largely ignored Untermann's explanations.

5. Jack London, *The Road* (New York: Greenberg, 1907), 9; hereafter cited as *Road*.

6. Franklin Dickerson Walker, *Jack London and the Klondike: The Genesis of an American Writer* (San Marino, Calif.: Huntington Library, 1972), 14; hereafter cited as *Klondike*.

7. Jack London to Anna Strunsky, 26 December 1900, *The Letters of Jack London*, ed. Earle Labor, Robert C. Leitz III, and I. Milo Shepard (Stanford, Calif.: Stanford University Press, 1988), 229; hereafter cited as *Letters*.

8. For a detailed account of Jack London's reading, see David Mike Hamilton, *The Tools of My Trade: Annotated Books in Jack London's Library* (Seattle: University of Washington Press, 1986), introduction; hereafter cited as *Tools*.

9. Andrew Sinclair, *Jack: A Biography of Jack London* (New York: Harper and Row, 1977), 48.

2. Literary Influences

1. Letter to Marion Humble, 11 December 1914, *Letters*, 1392.

2. Jack London, *John Barleycorn* (New York: Century, 1913), 41.

3. See *Tools*, introduction.

4. See *Tools*, 300. See also *A Son of the Sun* (New York: Doubleday, Page, 1912), 184, and *Mutiny of the Elsinore* (London: Mills and Boon, 1915), 104. For London's reading Zola on the *Reindeer*, see Irving Stone, *Sailor on Horseback: The Biography of Jack London* (New York: Doubleday, 1977), 41.

5. See "Notes and Comments," *North American Review* 149 (July 1889): 118.

6. Thomas Bailey Aldrich, *The Sisters' Tragedy, with Other Poems, Lyrical and Dramatic* (Boston: 1891), 28.

7. See M. B. Jones, "Translations of Zola in the United States Prior to 1900," *Modern Language Notes* 55 (November 1940): 521; hereafter cited as "Translations."

8. See Emile Zola, preface, *l'Assomoir*.

9. Jones, "Translations," 522–23.

10. Stephen Crane to John Northern Hilliard, January 1896, *Stephen Crane: Letters*, ed. R. W. Stallman and Lillian Gilkes (New York: New York University Press, 1960), 109–10.

11. See Earle Labor, introduction, *Jack London: A Trilogy: "All Gold Cañon," "The Night Born," "The Red One"* (Glen Ellen, Calif.: Jack London Research Center).

12. Charmian London, *The Book of Jack London*, 2 vols. (New York: Macmillan, 1921), 2:323.

4. International Critical Reception

1. Jack London to George P. Brett, 10 March 1903, *Letters*, 351.

2. Arthur Bartlett Maurice, "Jack London and *The Call of the Wild*," *Bookman* (October 1903): 155; anonymous reviewer, "*The Call of the Wild*," *Athenaeum* (1903): 279.

3. Anonymous, "Literary Table: Glimpses of New Books," *Current Literature* 35 (1903): 369.

4. William Morton Payne, "Recent Fiction [*The Call of the Wild*]," *The Dial* 35 (October 1903): 261.

5. Kate B. Stille, "Review of *The Call of the Wild*," *Book News Monthly* 22 (1903): 8.

6. Anonymous, "Books Old and New," *Atlantic Monthly* 92 (1903): 582.

Notes and References

7. Anonymous, *Charleston News*, 9 August 1903.

8. Mary Holland Kinkaid, (*Milwaukee*) *Sentinel*, 24 July 1903.

9. Anonymous, *Louisville Courier Journal*, 25 July 1903.

10. George Hamlin Fitch, *San Francisco Chronicle*, 2 August 1903.

11. Roderick Nash, introduction, *The Call of the Wild* (New York: George Braziller, 1970), 2. See also Earl Wilcox, "Jack London's Naturalism: The Example of *The Call of the Wild*," *Jack London Newsletter* 2 (1969).

12. John Perry, *Jack London: An American Myth* (Chicago: Nelson-Hall, 1981), 132.

13. See *Jack*, 74–75, and Joan D. Hedrick, *Solitary Comrade: Jack London and His Work* (Chapel Hill: University of North Carolina Press, 1982), 102; hereafter cited as *Comrade.*

14. Raymond Benoit, "Jack London's *The Call of the Wild*," *American Quarterly* 20 (Summer 1968): 247.

15. Pierre Berton, "Gold Rush Writing," *Canadian Literature* (1960): 59–67, and *Times*, 253.

16. Andrew Flink, "*Call of the Wild*: Jack London's Catharsis," *Jack London Newsletter* 11 (1978): 12–19; and "*Call of the Wild*: The Parental Metaphor," *Jack London Newsletter* 7 (1974): 57–62.

17. See *Times*, 252, and Carolyn Johnston, *Jack London: An American Radical?* (Westport, Conn.: Greenwood Press, 1981), 81.

18. Hensley C. Woodbridge, "Into What Languages Has London Been Translated," *Jack London Newsletter* 8 (1975): 84.

19. For a detailed list, see Hensley C. Woodbridge's unpublished "A Survey of Book Length Translations of the Works of Jack London Based on the *Index Translationum*, 1975–1985."

20. Vil Bykov, "A Manly Talent," *Komsomol Pravda*, 20 and 23 September 1959 (newspaper article commemorating the fortieth anniversary of London's death). Translator Robert Johnston's manuscript is at the Huntington Library, San Marino, Calif.

21. Deming Brown, *Soviet Attitudes Toward American Literature* (Princeton, N.J.: Princeton University Press, 1962), 220.

22. Nadezhda K. Krupskya, *Memories of Lenin* (New York, 1930), 208–9.

23. Carlos Daghlian, "Jack London in Brazil and Portugal," *Jack London Newsletter* 8 (1975): 22.

24. Arnold Chapman, *The Spanish American Reception of United States Fiction* (Berkeley: University of California Press, 1966), 49.

25. Olga P. Orechwa, "Review of Jerzy Szkup, *Recepcja Prozy Amerykanskiej W Polsce Ludowej W Latah: 1945–65*," *Jack London Newsletter* 8 (1975): 6–8.

26. Carl Anderson, *The Swedish Acceptance of American Literature* (Philadelphia: University of Pennsylvania Press, 1957), 38.

27. Mary Sue Schriber, "London in France, 1905–1939," *American Literary Realism* 9 (1976): 171–77.

28. Jack London to Robert Lutz, 1 October 1909, *Letters*, 836.

29. Jack London to Hughes Massie, 17 March 1914, *Letters*, 1309.

30. Anne M. Springer, *The American Novel in Germany: A Study of the Critical Reception of Eight Novelists Between the Two World Wars* (Hamburg: Cram, de Gruyter, 1960), 32–33, and Lawrence Marsden Price, *The Reception of United States Literature in Germany* (Chapel Hill: University of North Carolina Press, 1966), 130–32.

31. *The Call of the Wild* was translated into Japanese for the first time in 1917 and was the first of London's books to be used as a textbook of English by Takeo Arishima, one of the famous novelists of modern Japan, for the students of Hokkaido University. The "Society of [The Call of] the Wild" was established there in 1908. See Sachito Nakada, "Jack London and the Japanese Reader, Now and Then," *Jack London Echoes*, 2:2 (1982): 16–17.

32. Li Shuyan, "Jack London in China," *Jack London Newsletter* 19 (1986): 42–46.

33. *Foreign Literature Studies* 4 (1984).

5. A Dream of Freedom

1. See London's letter to Eliza Shepard, contained in his letter to Corinne Maddern, from Seoul, Korea, 4 April 1904 (Huntington Library, San Marino, Calif.), file MI 770.

2. See London's description of the ideal man-comrade in his letter to Charmian Kittredge, July 1903, *Letters*, 370–71.

3. Jack London to Caroline Sterling, 15 September 1905, *Letters*, 524.

4. Jack London to Caroline Sterling, 15 September 1905, *Letters*, 520–21.

5. Jack London to Charmian Kittredge, early July 1903, *Letters*, 372.

6. Illustration in *Letters*, vol. 2, 944–45.

7. Jack London to Charmian Kittredge, 18 June 1903, *Letters*, 365.

8. Jack London to Cloudesley Johns, 15 March 1899, *Letters*, 60.

9. See Clarice Stasz, *American Dreamers: Charmian and Jack London* (New York: St. Martin's Press, 1988), 57.

10. Jack London to Ninetta Eames, 3 April 1900, *Letters*, 178.

11. Jack London to Anna Strunsky, 6 April 1900, *Letters*, 179.

12. Jack London to Anna Strunsky, 10 June 1902, *Letters*, 298.

13. Jack London to Anna Strunsky, 25 August 1902, *Letters*, 307.

14. Jack London to Caroline Sterling, 15 September 1905, *Letters*, 521.

15. Jack London to Anna Strunsky, 16 and 21 August 1902, *Letters*, 305–6.

16. Jack London to Anna Strunsky, 28 August 1902, *Letters*, 309.

17. *The People of the Abyss*, in Jack London, *Novels and Social Writings* (New York: Library of America, 1982), 182.

18. Ernest Untermann to Joan London, 22 January 1938 (Huntington Library, San Marino, Calif.), file MI 1202.

19. Jack London, *The People of the Abyss*, 164.

20. Ernest Untermann to Joan London, 8 April 1938 (Huntington Library, San Marino, Calif.), file MI 1204.

6. A Tale of Devolution

1. Jack London Manuscript Collection (Huntington Library, San Marino, Calif.), file JL 7153.

2. See Jacqueline Tavernier-Courbin, ed., "Notes and Documents," *Critical Essays on Jack London* (Boston: G. K. Hall, 1983), 269.

3. Letter to Cloudesley Johns, 23 June 1899, *Letters*, 88.

4. Jack London Manuscript Collection (Huntington Library, San Marino, Calif.), file 745.

5. "These Bones Shall Rise Again," *The Reader* (June 1903), reprinted in *Jack London: No Mentor But Myself*, ed. Dale L. Walker (Port Washington, N.Y.: Kennikat Press, 1978), 71; hereafter cited as *Mentor*.

6. *Impressions* (November 1901), in *Mentor*, 40–41.

7. "Stranger than Fiction," *The Critic* (August 1903), in *Mentor*, 73.

8. "Getting into Print," *The Editor* (March 1903), in *Mentor*, 57.

9. See letter to Mabel Applegarth from Dyea Beach, 8 August 1897, *Letters*, 11.

10. Jack London, *A Daughter of the Snows* (Philadelphia: J. B. Lippincott Company, 1902), 117.

11. See, in particular, Marshall Bond's manuscript (Huntington Library, San Marino, Calif.), file JL 33; Fred Thompson's diary of his Yukon experience with Jack London (Huntington Library), file FAC 901; and Emil Jensen's "Jack London at Stewart River" (Huntington Library), file JL 144.

12. See Jack London Manuscript Collection (Huntington Library, San Marino, Calif.), file JL 33. The original of this manuscript is at the Beinecke Library, Yale University, New Haven, Conn.

13. *Letters*, 399.

14. *Impressions* (June 1901), in *Mentor*, 35.

15. Letter to Anna Strunsky, 20 December 1902, *Letters*, 328–29.

16. Jack London, *The Son of the Wolf* (London: Arco Publications, 1962), 46.

7. Buck and Carl Jung's Archetypes of the Collective Unconscious

1. See in particular Frieda Fordham, *An Introduction to Jung's Psychology* (Harmondsworth, Eng.: Penguin, 1970), 19; hereafter cited as *Jung*. See also *Psyche and Symbol: A Selection from the Writings of C. G. Jung*, ed. Violet S. de Laszlo (Garden City, N.Y.: Doubleday Anchor Books, 1958), hereafter cited as *Psyche*; and *Man and His Symbols*, ed. and intro. Carl G. Jung (New York: Dell, 1969), hereafter cited as *Man*.

2. C. G. Jung, from *Aion*, reprinted in part in *Psyche*, 3; hereafter cited as *Aion*.

3. From C. G. Jung's commentary on *The Secret of the Golden Flower*, in *Psyche*, 308.

4. Quoted in *Jung's*, 48.

5. C. G. Jung, "Approaching the Unconscious," in *Man*, 34; hereafter cited as "Approaching."

6. See J. A. Hall, *The Jungian Experience: Analysis and Individuation* (Toronto: Inner City Books, 1986), 47.

7. M. L. von Franz, "The Process of Individuation," in *Man*, 220.

8. Jack London to Merle Maddern, 28 August 1903, in *Letters*, 381.

8. Buck as Mythical Hero

1. Denis de Rougemont, *Love in the Western World* (New York: Fawcett, 1966), 18–19.

2. Joseph Campbell, *The Hero with a Thousand Faces* (New York: Meridian, 1956), 19. Further quotations are from pages 55, 82, 97, and 109.

3. See Maxwell Geismar, *Rebels and Ancestors: The American Novel, 1890–1915* (Boston: Houghton Mifflin, 1953), 150–51.

4. Charles N. Watson, *The Novels of Jack London: A Reappraisal* (Madison: University of Wisconsin Press, 1983), 47.

5. See, for example, *The Call of the Wild*, 49, 71, 81, 136, 139.

6. James Glenn Cooper, "A Womb of Time: Archetypal Patterns in the Novels of Jack London," excerpt from ch. 2, "The Hero," *Jack London Newsletter* 9 (1976): 16–28, and another excerpt under the same title in *Jack London Newsletter* 12 (1979): 12–23.

7. Ann Upton, "The Wolf in the Mirror," *Jack London Newsletter* 6 (1973): 111–18; reprinted in *The Call of the Wild*, ed. Earl Wilcox (Chicago: Nelson-Hall, 1980).

8. Raymond Benoit, "Jack London's *The Call of the Wild*," *American Quarterly* 20 (1968): 246.

9. See D. H. Lawrence, *Studies in Classical American Literature* (New York: Viking Press, 1964), 63. The actual quotation is, of course, about Deerslayer and reads: "A man who turns his back on white society. A man who keeps his moral integrity hard and intact. An isolate, almost selfless, stoic, enduring man, who lives by death, by killing, but who is pure white."

9. A Romantic Novel

1. Paul Valéry, "Situation de Baudelaire," *Revue de France* 5 (15 September 1924): 224.

2. Mario Praz, *The Romantic Agony* (Oxford University Press, 1933); excerpt entitled "The Romantic Sensibility," reprinted in *Romanticism: Points of View* (Englewood Cliffs, N.J.: Prentice-Hall, 1970), 82–95; hereafter cited as *Romanticism*.

3. See Frank Norris, "A Plea for Romantic Fiction," *Boston Evening Transcript*, 18 December 1901, 14; reprinted in *The Literary Criticism of Frank Norris*, ed. Donald Pizer (Austin: University of Texas Press, 1964), 75–78, hereafter cited as *Norris*.

4. Frank Norris, "Zola as a Romantic Writer," *San Francisco Wave* 15 (27 June 1896): 3, reprinted in *Norris*, 72.

5. Quoted in *Romanticism*, 89.

6. Alfred Kazin, *On Native Grounds* (New York, 1942), 110.

7. Jack London, "The Terrible and Tragic in Fiction," in *Mentor*, 61, 63.

8. Primo Levi, *The Mirror Maker: Stories and Essays* (New York: Schocken Books, 1989), 151.

9. See Clarice Stasz, "Androgyny in the Novels of Jack London," *Western American Literature* 11 (1976): 121–33.

10. Letter to John R. Lindmark, 21 September 1915, *Letters*, 1504.

11. Jack London, "In a Far Country," in *Short Stories of Jack London*, ed. Earle Labor, Robert C. Leitz III, and I. Milo Shepard (New York: Macmillan, 1990), 32; hereafter cited as *Short*.

12. Jack London, "To Build a Fire," in *Short*, 283.

Selected Bibliography

Primary Sources

Works by Jack London

The Son of the Wolf. Boston: Houghton Mifflin, 1900.

The God of His Fathers. New York: McClure Phillips, 1901.

Children of the Frost. New York: Macmillan, 1902.

The Cruise of the Dazzler. New York: Century, 1902.

A Daughter of the Snows. Philadelphia: J. B. Lippincott, 1902.

The Call of the Wild. New York: Macmillan, 1903.

The Kempton-Wace Letters (with Anna Strunsky). New York: Macmillan, 1903.

The People of the Abyss. New York: Macmillan, 1903.

The Faith of Men. New York: Macmillan, 1903.

The Sea-Wolf. New York: Macmillan, 1904.

The Game. New York: Macmillan, 1905.

Tales of the Fish Patrol. New York: Macmillan, 1905.

War of the Classes. New York: Macmillan, 1905.

Moon-Face and Other Stories. New York: Macmillan, 1906.

Scorn of Women. New York: Macmillan, 1906.

White Fang. New York: Macmillan, 1906.

Before Adam.. New York: Macmillan, 1907.

Love of Life and Other Stories. New York: Macmillan, 1907.

The Road. New York: Macmillan, 1907.

The Iron Heel. New York: Macmillan, 1908.

Martin Eden. New York: Macmillan, 1909.

Burning Daylight. New York: Macmillan, 1910.

Lost Face. New York: Macmillan, 1910.

Revolution and Other Essays. New York: Macmillan, 1910.

Theft: A Play in Four Acts. New York: Macmillan, 1910.

Adventure. New York: Macmillan, 1911.

The Cruise of the Snark. New York: Macmillan, 1911.

South Sea Tales. New York: Macmillan, 1911.

When God Laughs and Other Stories. New York: Macmillan, 1911.

The House of Pride and Other Tales of Hawaii. New York: Macmillan, 1912.

Smoke Bellew. New York: Century, 1912.

A Son of the Sun. Garden City, N.Y.: Doubleday, Page, 1912.

The Abysmal Brute. New York: Century, 1913.

John Barleycorn. New York: Century, 1913.

The Night-Born. New York: Century, 1913.

The Valley of the Moon. New York: Macmillan, 1913.

The Mutiny of the Elsinore. New York: Macmillan, 1914.

The Strength of the Strong. New York: Macmillan, 1915.

The Scarlet Plague. New York: Macmillan, 1915.

The Star Rover. New York: Macmillan, 1915. Published in England as *The Jacket*.

The Acorn-Planter: A California Forest Play. New York: Macmillan, 1916.

The Little Lady of the Big House. New York: Macmillan, 1916.

The Turtles of Tasman. New York: Macmillan, 1916.

The Human Drift. New York: Macmillan, 1917.

Jerry of the Islands. New York: Macmillan, 1917.

Michael, Brother of Jerry. New York: Macmillan, 1917.

The Red One. New York: Macmillan, 1918.

On the Makaloa Mat. New York: Macmillan, 1919.

Hearts of Three. New York: Macmillan, 1920.

Dutch Courage and Other Stories. New York: Macmillan, 1922.

The Assassination Bureau, Ltd. (completed by Robert Fish). New York: McGraw-Hill, 1963.

Letters from Jack London. Edited by King Hendricks and Irving Shepard. Odyssey, N.Y.: Doubleday, 1965.

Jack London Reports. Edited by King Hendricks and Irving Shepard. Garden City, N.Y.: Doubleday, 1970.

Daughters of the Rich. Edited by James E. Sisson. Oakland, Calif.: Holmes Book Co., 1971.

Jack London's Articles and Short Stories for the (Oakland) High School Aegis. Edited by James E. Sisson. Grand Rapids, Mich.: Wolf House Books, 1971.

Gold (with Herbert Heron). Edited by James E. Sisson. Oakland, Calif.: Holmes Book Co., 1972.

No Mentor but Myself. Edited by Dale L. Walker. Port Washington, N.Y.: Kennikat Press, 1979.

The Letters of Jack London. 3 vols. Edited by Earle Labor, Robert C. Leitz, and I. Milo Shepard. Stanford, Calif.: Stanford University Press, 1988.

Short Stories of Jack London. Edited by Earle Labor, Robert C. Leitz III, and I. Milo Shepard. New York: Macmillan, 1990.

The Complete Short Stories of Jack London. 3 vols. Edited by Earle Labor, Robert C. Leitz III, and I. Milo Shepard. Stanford, Calif.: Stanford University Press, 1993.

Selected Secondary Sources

Books

Beauchamp, Gorman. *Jack London*. Mercer Island: Wash.: Starmont House, 1984.

Freeman, A. W. *A Search for Jack London*. Chicago: Adams Press, 1973. A personal interpretation offering biographical information and criticism excerpted or derived from other published sources. Prefers London's later books with socialistic or mythic motifs. Sees London as a humanist and writer of the "common people."

Hamilton, David Mike. *"The Tools of My Trade": Annotated Books in Jack London's Library*. Seattle: University of Washington Press, 1986. A very useful and well-documented book that traces the intellectual development of London through his reading.

Hedrick, Joan D. *Solitary Comrade: Jack London and His Work*. Chapel Hill: University of North Carolina Press, 1982. An interesting book linking much of London's work to his troubled relationship with his lower-class origins.

Hendricks, King. *Jack London: Master Craftsman of the Short Story*. Logan: Faculty Association, Utah State, 1966. An excellent study emphasizing London's strong narrative, marvelous atmosphere, ironical situations, and dramatization of depth of human tragedies.

Kingman, Russ. *Jack London: A Definitive Chronology*. Los Angeles: David Rejl, 1992. A detailed, almost day-by-day chronology based on both published and unpublished sources.

Labor, Earle. *Jack London*. New York: Twayne Publishers, 1974. An excellent pioneer study of London's work which emphasizes its mythical characteristics. Must be read.

Labor, Earle, and Jeanne Cambell Reesman. *Jack London, Revised Edition*, New York: Twayne Publishers, 1994. This study, a revision of the pathbreaking 1973 Labor volume, gives extensive treatment to London's lesser-known work.

———, ed. *Jack London. Modern Fiction Studies* (1976), 22:1.

Lartemy, Eugene P., and Mary Ridge. *For Love of Jack London: His Life with Jennie Prentiss—A True Love Story*. New York: Vantage Press, 1991. A fictionalized account of the role played by Jennie Prentiss in Jack London's life.

Levi, Primo. *The Mirror Maker: Stories and Essays*. New York: Schocken Books, 1989. The essay "Jack London's Buck" is both interesting and amusing.

London, Charmian. *The Book of Jack London*. New York: Macmillan, 1921. A long, intimate, biography in two volumes providing a wealth of details on London's life, and his second marriage in particular.

London, Joan. *Jack London and His Times*. Seattle: University of Washington Press, 1968. A biography by London's elder daughter from a narrow socialistic point of view. It offers a lot of information on the social reality of the times, but it is rather prejudiced in its approach to London's brand of Socialism and his eventual withdrawal from the movement. She ignores much available information that would have clarified London's beliefs.

———. *Jack London and His Daughters*. Berkeley, Calif.: Heyday Books, 1990. A personal, one-sided document aimed at revealing London's failures as a father, which reveals indirectly Bessie Maddern's negative impact on the lives of her daughters. A biased and often inaccurate presentation of London as husband and father. Again, Joan London disregards facts and evidence that do not further her need to cast wholesale blame on her father.

Lundquist, James. *Jack London: Adventures, Ideas, and Fiction*. New York: Ungar, 1988.

McClintock, James I. *White Logic: Jack London's Short Stories*. Grand Rapids, Mich.: Wolf House Books, 1975. A valuable and perceptive study of London's career as a short-story writer showing London as a conscious artist who anticipated important themes in modern literature.

Martin, Stoddard. *California Writers: Jack London, John Steinbeck, the Tough Guys*. New York: St. Martin's, 1983. A well-written book that attempts to find a continuing strand of class struggle in Californian writing from London to Chandler. The section on London is neither properly researched nor adequately documented.

O'Connor, Richard. *Jack London: A Biography*. Boston: Little, Brown, 1964. It emphasizes London's adventures and dramatizes its subject, treating London as a celebrity rather than a serious writer. Some problems with documentation. O'Connor's dislike of London becomes obvious in the last sections. He dismisses London's major works in a series of superficial plot summaries and ignores his influence on American writing.

Ownbey, Ray Wilson. *Jack London: Essays in Criticism*. Santa Barbara, Calif.: Peregrine Smith, 1978. A very useful collection.

Perry, John. *Jack London: An American Myth*. Chicago: Nelson-Hall, 1981. An unbalanced and prejudiced biography consisting mainly of gossip and condemnations. Uses only unfavorable reviews and sources. Tries almost angrily to demolish the myths surrounding London's career but cannot explain away London's tremendous popularity.

Pizer, Donald. *Realism and Naturalism in Nineteenth-Century American Literature*. Carbondale: Southern Illinois University Press, 1984. The section on London, "The Problem of Form," divides London's works between fables and parables and finds a moral allegory in *The Call of the Wild* and *White Fang*.

Sinclair, Andrew. *Jack: A Biography of Jack London*. New York: Harper and Row, 1977. An interesting and readable biography from a Freudian perspective.

Springer, Bettina C. *"The Call of the Wild" by Jack London*. London: Althouse Press, 1986.

Stasz, Clarice. *American Dreamers: Charmian and Jack London*. New York: St. Martin's Press, 1988. A fascinating biography of London and Charmian's relationship offering some interesting insights into London's acceptance of androgyny and attitude toward women.

Stone, Irving. *Sailor on Horseback: The Biography of Jack London*. Boston: Houghton Mifflin, 1938. A less-than-reliable biography of London that makes little distinction between fact and fiction and does not indicate its sources.

Tavernier-Courbin, Jacqueline, ed. *Critical Essays on Jack London*. Boston: G. K. Hall, 1983. A major annotated collection of criticism also offering a selection of unpublished London manuscripts as documentation for the critical essays.

———, ed. *The Humor of Jack London*. *Thalia: Studies in Literary Humor* (1992), 12:1, 2. A collection of essays on an aspect of London's work that remains largely unacknowledged.

Walcutt, Charles Child, ed. *Seven Novelists in the American Naturalist Tradition: An Introduction*. Minneapolis: University of Minnesota Press, 1974. Feels that London tried to live several lives at the same time and, in the process, sacrificed his life, his art, and his peace. Buck enacts "London's own myth" of the unloved, fatherless, and poverty-stricken child who survives through innate strength.

Walker, Dale. *The Alien Worlds of Jack London*. Wolf House Books Monograph No. 1. Grand Rapids, Mich.: Wolf House Books, 1973. An interesting study that discusses London's science fiction.

Walker, Franklin Dickerson. *Jack London and the Klondike: The Genesis of an American Writer*. San Marino, Calif.: Huntington Library, 1966. A fascinating and detailed study of London's experiences in the Klondike and of their dramatization in his works. A model of objective criticism.

Watson, Charles N. *The Novels of Jack London: A Reappraisal*. Madison: University of Wisconsin Press, 1983. An interesting book demonstrating London's dependence on personal experience in his writings.

Special issue on Jack London. *Western American Literature* (1976), 11:2.

Williams, Tony. *Jack London. The Movies. An Historical Survey*. Los Angeles: David Rejl, 1992. A well-illustrated and well-researched discussion of London's relationship with the movie industry, as well as a discussion of the movies made on his work in America and abroad.

Zamen, Mark E. *Standing Room Only: Jack London's Controversial Career as a Public Speaker*. New York: Peter Lang, 1990. A readable and well-researched book.

Articles

Baskett, Sam S. "Jack London's Heart of Darkness." *American Quarterly* 10 (September 1958): 66–77.

Benoit, Raymond. "Jack London's *The Call of the Wild*." *American Quarterly* 20 (Summer 1968): 246–48.

Berton, Pierre. "Gold Rush Writing." *Canadian Literature* (1960): 59–67.

Brooks, Van Wyck. "Frank Norris and Jack London," in *The Confident Years, 1885–1915*. New York: Dutton, 227–37.

Clayton, Lawrence. "The Ghost Dog, A Motif in *The Call of the Wild*." *Jack London Newsletter* 5 (1972): 158.

Cooper, James Glenn. "A Womb of Time: Archetypal Patterns in the Novels of Jack London." *Jack London Newsletter* 9 (1976): 16–28.

Flink, Andrew. "*The Call of the Wild*: Jack London's Catharsis." *Jack London Newsletter* 11 (1978): 12–19.

———. "*The Call of the Wild*: Parental Metaphor." *Jack London Newsletter* 7 (1974): 57–62.

Frey, Charles. "Contradiction in *The Call of the Wild*." *Jack London Newsletter* 12 (1979): 35–37.

Labor, Earle. "Jack London's Mondo Cane: *The Call of the Wild* and *White Fang*." *Jack London Newsletter* 1 (1967): 2–13.

MacDonald, Marie. "On Rereading Jack London." *Jack London Newsletter* 15 (1982): 37–39.

Maffi, Mario. "The Law of Life: Jack London and the Dialectic of Nature." *Jack London Newsletter* 12 (1979): 42–46.

Munn, John. "The Theme of the Double in *The Call of the Wild.*" *Markham Review* 8 (1978): 1–5.

Naso, Anthony J. "Jack London and Herbert Spencer." *Jack London Newsletter* 14 (1981): 13–34.

Pankake, Jon Alan. "The Broken Myths of Jack London: Civilization, Nature and the Self in the Major Works." *Dissertation Abstracts International,* 36–5301 A.

Peterson, Clell T. "London and Lorenz: A Brief Note on Men and Dogs." *Jack London Newsletter* 12 (1979): 46–49.

Richler, Mordecai. "Dogs and Wolves." *Spectator* (1963): 211.

Shivers, Alfred S. "The Romantic in Jack London: Far Away from the Frozen Wilderness." *Alaskan Review* 1 (1936): 38–47.

Skipp, Francis E. "A Survey of Jack London Criticism." *American Literary Realism* 8 (1975): 299.

Spinner, Jonathan H. "A Syllabus for the 20th Century: Jack London's *The Call of the Wild.*" *Jack London Newsletter* 7 (1974): 73–78.

Stephane, Nelly. "L'Homme sauvage et le loup domestique." *Europe,* 561–622: 108–13.

Tanner, Tony. "*The Call of the Wild.*" *Spectator* (1965): 80–81.

Wilcox, Earl J. "Jack London's Naturalism: The Example of *Call of the Wild.*" *Jack London Newsletter* 2 (1969): 91–101.

———. "'The Kipling of the Klondike': Naturalism in London's Early Fiction." *Jack London Newsletter* 6 (1973): 1–12.

Bibliographies and Bibliographical Articles

Baskett, Sam S. "A Brace for London Criticism: An Essay Review." *Modern Fiction Studies* 22 (1976): 101–5.

Haydock, James. "Jack London: A Bibliography of Criticism." *Bulletin of Bibliography* 23: 42–46.

Lachtman, Howard. "Criticism of Jack London: A Selected Checklist." *Modern Fiction Studies* 22 (1976): 107–25.

Sherman, Joan R. *Jack London: A Reference Guide.* Boston: G. K. Hall, 1977.

Sisson, James E., and Robert W. Martens. *Jack London First Editions: A Chronological Reference Guide.* Oakland, Calif.: Star River House, 1979.

Walker, Dale H. *The Fiction of Jack London: A Chronological Bibliography.* El Paso: Texas Western Press, 1972.

Index

Index

BOOKS

Before Adam, 19, 32
Burning Daylight, 32
Call of the Wild, The, 6, 8, 10, 20–22, 37, 42, 107–9; as adventure story, 20, 24; as allegory, 21, 24, 25, 63; as American Dream, 93–94; appeal of, 19, 20, 26; international readership of, 28–34; justice theme in, 107; as myth, 21–22, 26, 82–95; prose style of, 22; publication, 23–24; reviews of, 24–25; sales of, 24; suffering in, 44, 60; and the unconscious, 21, 63–79; as work of Romanticism, 99–109
God of His Fathers, The, 62
Iron Heel, The, 27, 33
John Barleycorn, 11
Kempton-Wace Letters, The, 41, 42
Martin Eden, 4, 8, 27, 32, 33, 41
Mutiny on the Elsinore, The, 12
People of the Abyss,The, 4, 44, 48
Road, The, 6
Sea-Wolf, The, 32, 40
Son of the Sun, A, 12, 32
Son of the Wolf, The, 32, 62; Malemute Kid in, 54, 62; originals of characters in, 53–55
South Sea Tales, 32
Star Rover, The, 9, 48
When God Laughs, 32
White Fang, 32, 33, 103

STORIES

"American Abyss, The," 9
"Apostate, The," 33
"Bâtard" ("Diable—a Dog,"), 23, 62, 77
"Chinago, The," 33
"Dream of Debs, The," 33
"Goliah," 45

"Housekeeping in the Klondike," 53
"In a Far Country," 53, 61, 105–6
"Law of Life," 62
"Love of Life," 29
"Piece of Steak, A," 33
"Red One, The," 19
"Relic of the Pliocene, A," 62
"To Build a Fire," 62, 106, 107
"Where the Trail Forks," 106
"White Silence, The," 106

London, Joan (daughter), 27, 28, 54, 111n4
Love, as theme in London's works, 22, 42, 50, 60–61, 86, 100–101
Lutz, Robert, 31

Mandalas, 75–76
Maurice, Arthur Bartlett, 24
Michaud, Régis, 31
Milton, John: *Paradise Lost*, 53
Morrell, Ed, 48
Myth, 80–95; archetypes of, 82
Myth of the Hero, 21–22, 26, 82–89, 90, 91, 92–93

Nash, Roderick, 26
Naturalism, literary, 12, 13, 15–19, 56, 60, 98; and Realism, 99. *See also* Realism, literary
Nietzsche, Friedrich, 9, 33
Norris, Frank, 12, 13, 55, 56; "The Responsibilities of the Novelist," 98
North, romance and soul of the, 22, 109

Oyster piracy, 5, 12

Panic of 1893, 4
Partington, Blanche, 39, 43

The Author

Educated in France, where she received her Ph.D. in American literature in 1970 at the University of Aix en Provence, Jacqueline Tavernier-Courbin is professor of English at the University of Ottawa, Canada.

Author of *Ernest Hemingway: L'éducation européenne de Nick Adams* (Paris: Didier, 1978) and *The Making of Myth: Ernest Hemingway's "A Moveable Feast"* (Boston: Northeastern University Press, 1991), she also edited *Critical Essays on Jack London* (Boston: G. K. Hall, 1983) and *The Humor of Jack London* (*Thalia: Studies in Literary Humor*, 1992). Shorter works include interviews and chapters in collections of critical essays such as *Ernest Hemingway: Papers of a Writer*, edited by Bernard Oldsey (New York: Garland, 1981), *Ernest Hemingway: The Writer in Context*, edited by James Nagel (Madison: University of Wisconsin Press, 1984), *Critical Essays on Jack London* and *Charles Chaplin*, edited by Adolphe Nysenholc (Berlin, N.Y.: Mouton de Gruyter, 1991), as well as some 40 articles in major scholarly journals.

She has also edited *Thalia: Studies in Literary Humor* for the past 15 years, including special issues on such topics as "Humor and Religion," "Le Théâtre de Boulevard," "Southern Humor," "Australian Humor," and "Canadian Humor."